WAYS OF PRAYER SERIES

Basil Pennington, OCSO

Consulting Editor

Volume 10

Prayer

An Adventure in Living

by

Bishop B. C. Butler

Michael Glazier, Inc.
Wilmington, Delaware

About This Book

The writings of B. C. Butler, Auxiliary Bishop in Westminster
and former Abbot of Downside, are distinguished by a stimu-
lating literary, intellectual and theological clarity. He has
written widely and well on many topics; and examples of his
fresh and memorable approach can be found in his books,
among which are *The Church & Infallibility*; *Why Christ?*; and
The Theology of Vatican II.

Bishop Butler is above all else a man of prayer. Two decades
ago his *Prayer: An Adventure in Living* was published in America
and England; and reading it became a formative experience for
many. The publication of this new edition, with some very
minor changes, is a tribute to the perennial worth of the work.
Its seasoned spiritual wisdom, its thoughtful insights and
helpful good sense will ably guide many in their life of prayer
today.

Published in 1983 by Michael Glazier, Inc.
1723 Delaware Avenue, Wilmington, Delaware 19806
and the Incorporated Catholic Truth Society,
38-40 Eccleston Square, London SW1V 1PD

Library of Congress Catalog Card Number: 82-81395
International Standard Book Number:
    Michael Glazier, Inc.: 0-89453-282-0
    CTS: 0-85183-500-7

Cover design by Lillian Brulc
Typography by Richard Rein Smith
Printed in the United States of America

CONTENTS

Acknowledgments

The germ of this book was three short articles contributed to *The Catholic Gazette*. I wish to thank the editor for permission to make use here of the matter therein contained.

My thanks are also due to the management of *The Clergy Review* for permission to republish (as an appendix to this volume) an article which appeared in that periodical in August, 1953. Despite the article's forbidding title it deals with the same subject as that of Chapters V and VI of this book; but it addressed itself originally to a clerical audience equipped with such knowledge of dogmatic theology as cannot be expected from all the laity.

†B. C. Butler

Preface

I am grateful to the publishers for undertaking a new edition of this little book. On re-reading it after twenty years, I wish to make two comments.

First, the book speaks of "attending to God". It should be remembered that God is the ultimate Mystery, and that therefore our "attention" to him in prayer never results in a total understanding of him. The closest we get to understanding the uncreated Mystery is our understanding of his incarnate Word, Jesus Christ. And Christ, since his Ascension and the first Christian Pentecost, is always "available" to us.

Secondly, the beatific vision itself will still leave the ultimate Mystery unplumbed. As St. Gregory of Nyssa tells us, the Bliss of heaven will always be a joy to be more and more deeply penetrated but never exhausted.

†B. C. Butler.
31 August 1982.

Foreword

This short book is not a study of the theory of prayer, but an introduction to its practice. It is offered to the public in the hope that it may be read by some of those very many people who would be willing to embark on the adventure of prayer if they could convince themselves that this adventure is not the privilege of monks and nuns, of the professionally religious, or at least of people with a special 'gift' or an extraordinary call from God, but is genuinely possible for such as they, ordinary unassuming busy folk, yet faced, as we all are, by the immeasurable mystery of existence and the need to take up some position in the face of that mystery. In writing it, I have of course written as a Catholic, convinced that we all need the support and guidance, in the life of the spirit, of a guaranteed tradition and an authority that comes from above. But I have had in mind not only Catholic readers but others, of differing traditions, even such as so far have given their allegiance to no religious tradition. Most agnostics do not read books on prayer — the more's the pity. But I would hope that even an agnostic, if this book should fall into his hands, would catch some glimpse of the meaning which it tries to express, and would judge it no betrayal of his intellectual integrity to feel that it would be good if these things could be found to be true.

There are those who argue that there is something selfish about devoting one's life, or a large part of it, to the practice of the sort of prayer with which this book, after a few introductory chapters, comes to concern itself almost exclusively. It may be all very fine, they would say, to seek the personal happiness which may be hoped for from such devotion. Meanwhile, the world waits for the practical help of all men of good will. To go apart and pray, 'the world forgetting, by the world forgot', is the great refusal of the challenge of history.

My own conviction is, that precisely the opposite is true. The great need of Western Man at the present day is for a recovery of the tradition and the widespread practice of prayer. My mind's ear is always ringing with the Roman poet's criticism of those who, for the sake of living, surrender all that makes life worth while. Ringing, too, with the reiterated question of St Ignatius of Loyola to his young friend's forecast of the stages of his own future career: 'And then?' When we have perfected our techniques of education and art and production, including the production of the means to destroy our world, what then? For what purposes of expression or communication shall we use our artistic techniques? For what sort of life shall we educate? What and why shall we produce? What is the end that makes human living worth while? If we turn our back on the great spiritual tradition of mankind, instead of trying to develop it, what are we proposing to put in its place?

But if we accept the message of tradition, we accept the truth that life is for the sake of the good life, and that the good life is the life of the spirit. And we concede that the life of the spirit, in individuals and in society, burns in its purest essence in the life of prayer. The bonds that unite each of us, even the most solitary, with the life of society are both visible and invisible, strong and inescapable. No one can pursue the life of prayer, within the context of a whole life of dedication to God, the Supreme Good, and to his will, without exerting an influence on society. The health of society flows from this personal dedication and this influence. We Westerners of the twentieth century have inherited all the activism of our Indo-European ancestors. But we have largely discarded the ingredient of non-Aryan spirituality which gave depth and significance to our own more recent past. India, at least, still offers a synthesis — unsatisfactory for many reasons which need not be detailed here — of Indo-European activism with Oriental spirituality. I am not an advocate of Indian mysticism for Western Man; on the contrary I am an advocate of Christian mysticism for India. But India today still stands as a living reproach to our own abandonment of what is best in our Western past.

These are momentous issues, and they may seem somewhat remote to some who, I hope, may be encouraged by the following pages to find an answer to their own pressing needs in the life of prayer.

i

Presuppositions

We communicate our mind and our meaning to others by conversation and letter-writing. It is commonly held that we use prayer similarly to communicate our mind and meaning to God. By prayer we make God the confidant of our heart and our desires. As a preliminary to the subject of prayer it therefore seems reasonable to reflect about God and our relation to him.

Each of us, in the passing moment which is all that he has at his immediate disposal, is caught in a spider's web of circumstance. His present situation, the context of things and events in which he lives and has to act, is made up of factors which are not of his own choice or contriving; at least not of his present contriving, though some of these factors are consequences of his past decisions.

The factors of the present situation throng in upon him from all sides, constraining him, limiting his field of vision and his range of action. There are secondary, partial, patterns in this web of circumstances. Some of them, for instance, are things which arrange themselves, or can be arranged, in a framework of space and of time, in which they are related not only to the man whose situation they construct, but to one another. There are other factors, as for instance kindred, friends, fellow-citizens, fellow-Christians, which go to build up various moral wholes. And some factors bring into our experience some pattern of natural or moral beauty, or some element of scientific truth. But these are all patterns of a secondary kind, subsidiary instances of rationality within an incoherent totality of the whole situation. As a whole, my experience imprisons me in the incoherence of brute fact. What but my long familiarity with my human lot could dull my astonished and indignant protest at this inescapable imprisonment in sheer irrationality?

The web of circumstance, then, comprises my external world of things and of other persons. It also includes what may be called the internal factors of my own self, with its burden of the past and its desires or forebodings for the future. It includes my temperament, my formed habits and memories, subconscious urges, and instincts loaded with an unmeasured evolutionary pre-history; my mood, emotions and passions: fear or hope, longing or repugnance, burning with a steady fire beyond my control, or flaring up in sudden explosions of violence. All these, which we may count as internal factors when compared with 'the world out there', are still external to myself as I crave here and now for rationality, as I move towards the inevitable exercise of my power of free decision.

All of it, the outside factors and the internal factors, add up to nothing rational.

I myself, my most intimate 'I', am the product of unnumbered accidents. What random sequence of chances first brought my mother across my father's path? Through what hazardous interplay of circumstances did *their* respective parents meet? And so back again along a series of such accidents till we reach that fortuitous complex of chances that gave birth to the first living cell on a planet that broke off, perhaps, by a most improbable chance from the mass of a casual sun.

Like the web of circumstances in which I am caught today, I myself, then, add up to nothing rational. My roots are in accident; I swim in absurdity.

And yet, on the other hand, I am such that I cannot rest in irrationality. Irrationality is that which defies understanding; and I have — you might almost say I *am* — an unrestricted desire to understand. Obviously, I must seek understanding in order to control my circumstances, so far as to obtain the satisfaction of basic biological urges for food and drink, for self-preservation. But my desire to understand is not sated by the satisfaction of any physical hunger. On the contrary, it is just when my physical wants are satisfied, and I have time to think, that the desire to understand, the lure of wonder takes possession of my being and I am brought consciously face to face with the absurdity of my existence and my situation.

My intellectual dissatisfaction is matched by a practical perplexity. I have the power and the responsibility of free decision. As to this, we need not here enter into argument with the determinists. A man may think he has proved the impossibility of free will. But he has then to decide whether or not to shape his future decisions according to this philosophical opinion. The opinion may affect his decision of this grave issue, but the opinion itself is no substitute for the decision, which has to be made not by his intellect but by his will. We cannot escape from freedom.

But a decision of my will is an option for something judged to be 'worth while'. It is an act of self-committal to something apprehended as 'good' (not necessarily *morally* good; a good dinner is good, but in given circumstances it is not necessarily morally good). And since we are normally in this life presented with a choice between alternatives of action, the act of practical decision is normally a *preference* of one good rather than another (I choose to go for a walk *rather than* to read the newspaper). If my choice is to be rational — and I cannot escape from my natural desire for the rational — this act of preference must imply a scale of values, ultimately an *absolute good* to serve as a criterion by which to judge between particular limited good alternatives.

How can I have a scale of values in a situation which is basically irrational, ultimately absurd?

There is one answer to the demands of our intellect and the perplexities of our will: God. My situation is absurd if I leave God out of the picture. My revolt against absurdity is the expression of my desire for a total explanation; and God, infinitely wise, infinitely good, infinitely real, *is* the total explanation. As the printed works of Shakespeare are a meaningless collection of marks on paper, except when seen as a set of communications from a conscious intelligence to conscious intelligences, so my situation is meaningless, except when seen as an expression of the mind and will of God, addressed to me. The works of Shakespeare are full of meaning, but if they are to have a meaning for me I must take account of Shakespeare himself. My situation is full of meaning, but not if I refuse to take account of God. Shakespeare is not an optional extra to my understanding of the plays. God is not an optional extra to my understanding of my situation.

But if this is so, then we must take God seriously.

There is a story that St Thomas Aquinas, as a child at school, faced his schoolmaster with the question: *What is God?* Could any question be more interesting? Could any question be more difficult to answer adequately?

The odd thing is that in a sense we all, perhaps, know the answer to Thomas's question; yet it is an answer which we should find it hard to state. 'I understand, provided you don't ask me to explain.' It is a curious kind of knowledge. It seems to equip us rather to answer 'no' to the false suggestions than 'yes' to the true ones. Still, it is already something to know that might is not right, or that man is not an angel. So perhaps we may take heart from the number and variety of the suggestions about God to which we can certainly give a negative reply.

Is God limited in his knowledge? Is it possible for anything, even the most secret impulses of our human heart, to lie hidden from God? We answer: certainly not. Nothing that has any faintest tint of ignorance can possibly be God.

Is God's wisdom limited? God is our heavenly Father. Human fathers are expected to be wise, but their wisdom is subject to all sorts of limitations. We are certain that there are no limits at all to God's wisdom.

Is God immoral, selfish, or capricious? Left to himself, man pictures God in his own image. And since man is morally imperfect, Browning's Caliban imagined his god Setebos to be morally imperfect too:

Oh, He hath made things worthier than Himself,
And envieth that, so helped, such things do more

Than He who made them! What consoles but this?
That they, unless through Him, do nought at all,
And must submit: what other use in things?
'Hath cut a pipe of pithless elder-joint
That, blown through, gives exact the scream o' the jay
When from his wing you twitch the feathers blue:
Sound this, and little birds that hate the jay
Flock within stone's throw, glad their foe is hurt:
Put case, such pipe could prattle and boast forsooth
'I catch the birds, I am the crafty thing,
I make the cry my maker cannot make
With his great round mouth; he must blow through mine!'
Would not I squash it with my foot? So He.

But even Caliban felt that there was something wrong about this theology. He asks why his god is so 'rough, cold and ill at ease':

Aha, that is a question! Ask, for that,
What knows the something over Setebos
That made Him.

The 'something over Setebos' is something whose existence we are bound to surmise because Setebos's moral imperfections disqualify Him.

Is God limited in his being in any way? We answer 'no'. We are certain that nothing that is subject to limitation of any kind can possibly be God.

Is there more than one God? Again the answer is 'no'. We have an obscure certainty that, if there were several gods, each of them would be limited by the fact that he was not what the other gods were. When we read of the 'gods amany' of the pagans, we know that the word 'god' did not convey to their minds what the word 'God' conveys to ours.

In other words, we reject from our notion of God anything that implies imperfection, whether of being, or of knowing, or of holiness, or of any other description. Some might say that we are more sure that God is not imperfect than we are sure that he exists. And to this extent, negatively so to speak, we know what we mean by God.

We can add one further 'no': God is not just an ideal. What do we mean by this? Well, take the notion of a straight line. An absolutely straight line is not found in nature. But we have the idea, or ideal, of a straight line, by reference to which we measure the divergences of natural 'lines' from perfect straightness. But if it is suggested that God is just an ideal or an idea in that sense — something that need not exist, but is useful, as an idea, for the purpose of measuring the divergence of real things from perfection — we shall answer: No, that is not what we *mean* by God, any more than the mere idea of Shakespeare is what we mean by the author of the plays. By 'God' I mean something, someone, so utterly real that he is the very explanation and source of the (imperfect) reality of everything else, of everything that is and of everything that happens. He is the unplumbed, infinite, ocean of real positive being, knowledge, wisdom, power, holiness, love, joy. A mere idea of God would be at the opposite pole to what we mean by God. What we mean by God is something, someone, so real that we should see — if we could see the truth as God sees it — *that he could not possibly not* exist.

The trouble is, of course, that just when we start saying not negative but positive things about God, we come up against

formidable difficulties of thought and language. God is absolutely simple, with an infinitely rich simplicity. Hence, God's
wisdom, love, power, knowledge, being, are not a multiplicity
of qualities; they must be each identical with all the others,
identical with God himself. But a wisdom which *is* love, a love
which *is* justice, a wisdom, love, power, each of which *is* being
—these are inconceivable to us. It is impossible for us to have
an adequate, coherent, positive, conception of what we mean
by God, the infinite being.

Thus, at the very moment when we seek to pass from our
denials about God to affirm something positive about him, we
find that we are overcome by a sort of mental stammer that
rapidly develops into something like dumbness. We begin to
glimpse a truth in the answer which St Thomas Aquinas, by
now a mature theologian and philosopher, gave to his old
childish question: 'What is God?' 'The highest knowledge', he
says, 'that we can have of God in this life is to know that we do
not know him.',

The intellectual issues raised by this state of things are
various and profound. We are not concerned with them here;
the less so, since the person who seeks God, as a lover seeks his
beloved, is actually delighted to find that God so far exceeds
his intellectual grasp. He has a deep conviction that anything
that could be fitted neatly into man's own rational categories
would be infinitely less than the Reality which has fascinated
his mind and will.

What we need to say, and what we can say —though it
must necessarily be in more or less metaphorical language —
is that God is 'beyond' and 'above' the highest concept we can
form of him. We take, for instance, the idea of beauty. We
recognise that some things are more beautiful than others. We

expand our idea of beauty out from the most imperfect glimmerings of beauty towards things more beautiful, things most ravishingly beautiful; and we see that our mind has been following a sort of ascending trail. And then we say: God is up above, the infinite Beyond towards which that trail tends, though it never arrives. So with wisdom, knowledge, goodness, power. In each case we can set up in our minds an ascending scale. The ascending line of each points upwards, onwards, towards infinity, the limitless, the 'inconceivable' — it points towards God. And all lines point towards God. Being itself is one of these 'graded' notions. There is more of being in a human than in an animalcule, more reality in an angel than in a human. God's being, which is identical with himself (he doesn't *have* being; he *is* being), is at that 'point at infinity' to which the ascending lines of beauty, goodness, wisdom, power converge.

Precisely because God is the infinite Beyond, he is infinitely near, infinitely present. Creatures are shut off from each other by their limitations. God is unlimited. Bolts and barriers do not shut him out, nor the incommunicable privacy of a person's heart. All creaturehood is bathed in God, sustained by God. We exist at this moment, and the situation which we face exists, because God is here and now pouring existence into it and us —expressing his own mind and will, expressing himself, in and as our situation and ourselves — more truly than Shakespeare expressed himself in his plays.

By nature, then, we are in a relation of utter exterior and interior dependence on God. Prayer puts us into personal relationship with him. It is the response of our free self-determination to the fact of God and his presence. If life is a matter of adaptation to environment, prayer, the spiritual life in act, is adaptation to our ultimate environment, which is the all-encompassing reality of God.

It is not necessary to be a Christian in order to pray. On the contrary, conversion to the Christian faith may well be the result of prayer, as in the case of Cornelius the centurion according to the Acts of the Apostles: 'Thy prayers and alms-deeds are recorded on high in God's sight. And now he would have thee send men to Joppa, to bring here one Simon, who is surnamed Peter. . . . And he [Peter] gave orders that they should be baptised in the name of the Lord Jesus Christ' (x, 4, 5, 48). Christian prayer, however, is conditioned by Christian faith, faith in that message of God which was 'made flesh' as Jesus Christ and has been committed to the Church to transmit to all men. This message teaches us that 'the everlasting love of his Godhead, through which he made thee and wrought thee when thou wert nought'[1] has not been content with the incomprehensible outpouring of love which is implied by creation. On the contrary, 'God so loved the world, that he gave up his only-begotten Son, so that those who believe in him may not perish, but have eternal life' (John iii. 16).

'No man has ever seen God; but now his only-begotten Son, who abides in the bosom of the Father, has himself become our interpreter' — has 'expounded' God to us (John i. 18). Jesus Christ is, in fact, 'the Word' of God, who 'abode at the beginning . . . with God' and 'was God', and who, in becoming man, did not cease to be what and where he eternally is; so that 'whoever has seen me' with the eyes of faith 'has seen the Father' (John xiv. 9). 'Through him we

---

[1] *The Cloud of Unknowing,* ch. 1.

have access to the Father' (Ephesians ii. 18), through him 'in whom the whole treasury of wisdom and knowledge is stored up' (Colossians ii. 3).

All Christian prayer is conditioned by this faith, and by that supernatural help, mediated to us through the Church and her sacraments, which theologians call grace. It is prayer, as the collects say, 'through Jesus Christ our Lord'; but its goal is the incomprehensible depths of the Godhead, revealed indeed in the Word made flesh, but infinitely transcending all that our intelligence can absorb of that revelation: 'For why, he may well be loved, but not thought. By love may he be gotten and holden; but by thought never.'[2]

In the pages that follow, the language used will often be that of a Christian writing for Christians. But it is hoped that the non-Christian reader will not find it too difficult to make the necessary mental adjustments to fit most of it to his own need.

Meanwhile, there is one puzzle which it may be convenient to clear up here. As was said at the beginning of this chapter, it is commonly held that we use prayer to communicate our mind and meaning to God. It may be asked: Why bother to do this, since we know that God, who already knows all things, knows what we would say to him before we say it? It is quite true, that God knows all that is and knows the possibility of all that is possible. But he does not know our prayer (as actual) unless we pray; because, unless we pray, our prayer does not exist. We do not pray in order to pass on to God information that is ours before (by our prayer) it becomes his. We pray in order, in so doing, to make actual a relationship of our will to his which is consonant with the fact of our utter dependence

[2]*The Cloud of Unknowing*, ch. 6.

on him, and this relationship of our will to his is something that he desires of us. When the disciples in the boat at sea cried 'Lord, save us, we are sinking' they were not telling God about an external situation of which he had been unaware; but they were making actual an internal situation, of willed dependence on his mercy, which was both called for by his love and was met by a further outpouring of his love.

ii

A Rule of Prayer

In order to pray, we have said, it is not necessary to be a Christian. Non-Christian Jews pray, and set Christians a very good example in the practice. Moslems pray. So do Hindus. Prayer is co-extensive with religious belief. The Israelites prayed in the times before Christ, and the Jewish Psalter is the great traditional Christian treasury of prayer. But the ancient pagans, like their modern successors, also prayed. Prayer, you might say, is the most natural thing in the world.

Here is a quotation from a modern historian of religion, writing about the religion, in days gone by, of a village in the Vaucluse:

> Religion was the framework of the life of this human group. Quite apart from major occasions, when the villager felt the need of winning heaven's favour, such occasions that is to say as birth, marriage, and death, he felt, more or less vaguely, that

his lot, in this little corner of the earth, did not wholly depend on his own efforts and crafts; that there was still a margin, where man depends on Unknown Forces. And so he felt that it was prudent and wise to get on good terms with these forces.

The historian of ancient religions, the ethnologist who studies the behaviour of 'primitive' peoples, perhaps even the pre-historian who tries to understand how the remotest human stocks thought and lived, all recognise analogous facts which may presuppose the same background of beliefs — I mean the belief in these Unknown Forces which decide about the fertility of man and his flocks and fields, about the success of the annual expeditions in quest of booty — in short about the prosperity or otherwise of a particular human group.[1]

In moments of peril or of urgent need, who would not cry out in his anguish: God, help me?

Loud is my cry to the Lord, the prayer I utter for the Lord's mercy, as I pour out my complaint before him, tell him of the affliction I endure. My heart is ready to faint within me, but thou art watching over my path... I look to the right of me, and find none to take my part; all hope of escape is cut off from me, none is concerned for my safety. To thee, Lord, I cry, claiming thee for my only refuge, all that is left me in this world of living men.[2]

The sad thing is, that many who are forced to their knees by disaster or peril rarely pray when things are going well. That is why times of war are often times of religious revival.

---

[1]A. J. Festugière, *Revue Biblique*, 1958, p. 79.
[2]Psalm cxli. 2-7.

Of both nations and individuals it can be said: 'When he threatened them with death, they would search after him, feel their need of God once more'[3]; but in prosperity they forget their need.

Prayer is not only the business of asking God for help and favours, though it includes such petitions. We can certainly ask for help in our worldly affairs and interests. We are taught on excellent authority to think of God as our heavenly Father. We are even taught, and we believe, that *God is love*. Love stoops to take an interest in the lowliest interests of the beloved. The schoolboy who used to solicit his confessor's prayers before a cricket match was following a perfectly sound instinct. We can also ask God for the help we need to be sorry for our wrongdoing, and to do his will more perfectly in the future. 'Give me chastity and continence' was the prayer of the young Augustine, even when he was still so far from his goal that he would fain add 'but not yet'.[4] The man who calls himself an agnostic can yet pray to the God who may exist for light to see and grace to follow the truth. Did not Lacordaire, before his conversion, pray: 'God, if there is a God, save my soul, if I have a soul'?

And as we can seek temporal and spiritual helps from God for ourselves, so we can seek them for others, for those we love and for those we think we hate, for those who evoke our sympathy and also for those who provoke our dislike or indignation; we can pray for all men, for those yet unborn and for those who have died before us: 'Give them, Lord, eternal rest, and let everlasting light shine upon them.' There is a vast

[3]Psalm lxxvii. 34.
[4]*Confessions*, VIII, vii.

network of prayer going up daily and hourly to God from the Church on earth, both in her official prayer or liturgy and in the private prayers of the faithful. It is a privilege of the children of the Church that they are called upon to take part in this great collaborative work of prayer, and that they know themselves to be sustained by it, helped by the prayers of innumerable people unknown to themselves, yet neither unloving nor unloved.

The word 'prayer', however, covers not only such petitionary prayer but all our 'speaking to God'. Our prayer ought certainly to include thanksgiving, both on our own behalf and on behalf of others. Chesterton once remarked on the sad plight of the unbeliever who thinks that there is no one whom he can thank for the good things of life. The Great Prayer of the Church, the Canon of the Mass, is basically an act of adoring praise, but also of thanksgiving: 'It is truly fitting and right . . . that we should always and everywhere give thanks to thee, Lord.'

Above all, prayer ought to include love and praise or adoration: 'We praise thee, Lord, on account of thy great glory.' God is not just an impersonal source of benefits; he is our supreme lord and master, and our heavenly Father. We ought not to behave as though he were merely a celestial automatic machine, from which to extract what we want by our petitions. If there are too few who ask help from God except in realised danger or imminent need, perhaps fewer still, in the ordinary routine of life, thank and praise him as they should.

The occasions for adoration, thanksgiving, and petition are as uncountable as the situations in which we find ourselves, since God is the inner meaning and the transcendent Cause of every situation, the lord and governor of history, the timeless background of the changing stage of life. We should give as much place as possible to spontaneous prayer, letting it develop easily and without strain out of our circumstances, till we come to live habitually in the communion of familiar, informal, intercourse with God. If our faith was stronger and our love of God more dominating we should accept all this not only as a theoretical truth but as a practical programme.

In fact, however, most of us are such weak, selfish, forgetful creatures that we need to fortify our programme of spontaneous prayer with a regular rule of prayer, suitable to our make-up and our circumstances, a rule which we resolve to stick to through thick and thin. To make such a rule is only to apply to the subject of our relations with God the realistic common sense which goes without question in other affairs of life. Thus, if we decide that we need to take physical exercise, we shall be foolish if we trust to uncalculated impulse. We shall 'make a rule' of a daily walk, or daily exercises, or regular athletic games; and we shall try to keep it. Rules are good things, provided we neither neglect them nor become their slaves.

To some extent, the Church herself provides a rule of prayer for Catholics, since she makes it our duty to go to Mass on Sundays and the great holy days. But obligatory Mass attendance can be considered as an element of public prayer, and at present we are concerned with our private prayer as individual human beings.

There is no commandment of God or law of the Church which makes it obligatory to say daily morning and evening prayers. In itself, then, it is not sinful to omit them, though in a given case it might be slothful and therefore sinful. But we hardly need to learn that there is something lacking in a day which has not been sanctified at its start by a few moments of communion with God. Nor should we feel happy about going to bed at night without a word of thanks to God for the blessings of the past day, without asking forgiveness for the day's sins and negligences, without a prayerful thought for those we love and all who need our prayers, and a commendation of ourselves to God 'now and at the hour of our death'.[5]

Our rule of prayer, then, will include both morning and evening prayers daily. This is especially important, since many people will find it extremely difficult to fit in any set prayer between these two points; such is the rush of modern life. Of course, a passing shaft of prayer can be sent up to God at almost any moment, and 'the more the merrier'. God is always attending to each of us, as though each of us were the only creature God had ever made; and he is glad when we, on our part, attend to him even for a passing instant. But it is not so easy to set a few minutes apart for uninterrupted prayer; and for many people this is, as a rule, most practicable in the morning and in the evening.

What shall be the pattern of our daily morning prayer? Of course, nothing could be better — if we can manage it — than to attend Mass. It is a wonderful experience to go into one of the great Dublin churches on any weekday morning, and see Mass after Mass being attended by crowds of laymen, women and children. How better could we hallow or sanctify our day than by imitating them?

But we must be practical. A vast number of people cannot

---

[5]So, too, a meal which does not begin with 'grace' or 'asking a blessing' ought to seem to us as something less than fully human — something like the feeding of the animals at the Zoo.

do this — and they ought not to do it, because they would be neglecting their duty if they did. But there are comparatively few who cannot spend two or three minutes praying in their bedroom before they go down to breakfast and out to work. How will they use this time? Books like the *Garden of the Soul* and the *Simple Prayer Book* can be very useful to some people, with their set forms of morning (and evening) prayer. But it is not necessary to use or follow a book. You can be as informal as you like (with reverence and humility) in speaking to your heavenly Father, to Jesus your redeemer, to the Holy Spirit who is love personified. And in fact, if we do use a book or our own set form of words, it is a good thing to devote part of our time to impromptu prayer, thanking God for particular blessings, or recommending to him our own or others' passing needs.

Normally, one's morning prayer might include these elements: (1) An act of praise of God, for example: 'Glory be to the Father and to the Son and to the Holy Spirit. Amen.'[6] (2) Thanking God for having kept us safe in body and soul through the night and for bringing us to the beginning of the adventure of another day. (3) Prayer for those who have any claim upon us, whether they are living or dead; and who on earth or in the Church Suffering has not some claim upon a

[6]'Amen', as used at the end of Christian prayers (e.g. the great Amen sung by the congregation at the end of the Canon of the Mass) probably means 'We confirm the contents of the preceding prayer. So be it.' It is a Hebrew or Aramaic word, preserved for us in the Greek New Testament, apparently used by Our Lord himself, and so linking us up with the primitive Church, with Jesus Christ, and with the Israel of Old Testament times. Christians value these links with their own past, which are like, for instance, the academic hoods worn by members of a university today, as they were worn by their predecessors in days gone by. By such links the church's days and generations are bound together in a bond of natural piety.

member of Christ? (4) Prayer for God's protection and help in the coming day, and especially for grace to serve him in it with love, gladness, and initiative. (5) Everything could then be summed up in the Our Father, followed by a brief act of spiritual communion.

It takes some time to set all this down on paper. But it does not take long to carry it out into practice. Lucky are those who can make their morning prayers something more than the minimum!

One practice may be specially recommended. It is what is known as the 'morning offering', and is a short form of prayer which can be said while dressing (or shaving): 'I offer thee, God, my life, and especially all I shall do or suffer today, to thy honour and glory and for the salvation of souls; give me grace to live today in the spirit of this offering.' The actual words of course do not matter; what matters is the intention of the will, the sincerity of the act.

So much for our morning prayer. The elements of our evening prayer may be as follows. (1) As before, an act of praise. (2) Thanksgiving for all the blessings of the past day. (3) A very short glance back over the day, not in order to congratulate ourselves on our successes, but to see how we have failed in our service of God and others; this will be followed by an equally short act of repentance and prayer for forgiveness. (4) Prayer for others. (5) Prayer for God's protection during the night, and for grace to get up promptly tomorrow, so that we may have time for our morning prayer! We may well wonder how many come to grief in their life of prayer and religion because they have a habit of not getting up promptly. Prayer goes; Mass (even obligatory Mass) may begin to go; we 'lose contact' with God; then the devil tells us, falsely, that the effort to put things right would be too great. Of course, we are all as weak as water. That is why it is a good thing to ask God's help in this very simple matter of getting up when the alarm clock wakes us.

The important thing about our daily prayers is regularity; not the obsessional regularity of the scrupulous, but the reasonable regularity which we aim at in the rest of our activities. If we are regular about our morning and evening prayers, it will become easier to pray spontaneously (with short 'shafts' of prayer, 'ejaculations' as they are sometimes called) during the day. And so we shall begin to enter into our heritage as children of God, as the friends of Christ.

Note I. Prayer and Modern Science

We are concerned, in these pages, not with the philosophy of prayer but with its practice. It is, however, probable that some people today are deterred from prayer because they think it is inconsistent with the teachings of modern science to ask God for favours which in fact are determined by the inevitable laws of cause and effect which science discovers in nature. To take a concrete example: What, it may be asked, is the use of praying for rain in a drought? It is true that science is not yet in a position to predict the weather with unfailing accuracy. But scientists will tell us that this is only because we lack some of the data of the problem and the ability to draw the conclusions which the complete data would infallibly contain. Tomorrow's weather, then, is already settled by today's meteorological conditions; in fact, it was settled by yesterday's conditions. So what difference can prayer make?

A reply to this difficulty may be offered at two different levels of thought. At the level of ordinary common sense, one may point out that we are ourselves continually changing the course of nature by the exercise of our free will. We erect breakwaters; we invent heavier-than-air flying machines; we split the atom. It is absurd to suggest that what we can do, God cannot.

At a deeper level of thought, it is to be observed that the 'laws of nature' approach full definiteness and inevitability in the same degree as they approximate to pure mathematical formulations. But if pure mathematical truth is perfectly determinate, it is also in the highest degree abstract. In its abstract purity, it is true with the truth of God himself; and it only binds God in the sense —which is no sense — in which God is 'bound' by his own nature.[7] The actual world is only one possible exemplification of mathematical truth 'translated' into concrete phenomena.

God is above time, and the prayers which we make today are known to God 'from all eternity'. They entered into God's 'plan' for creation 'from the first', and in his infinite wisdom he 'chose' that plan of events, and of the interrelation of events, which would manifest, among other things, the account which he takes eternally of the prayers of his children. As that plan is expressed in the 'musical key' of mathematics, human scientists can of course read mathematical truth in it. They do so by disregarding the full concreteness of phenomena; as though a mathematical physicist with no 'ear' for the beauty of mathematics were to report that all that he could find in a

---

[7]God is not 'bound' by his own nature because he *is* his own nature. His nature is one with his sovereign liberty of selfhood.

symphony of Beethoven was the precise conformity of the music to the scientific 'laws' of sound.

Note II. 'Unanswered' Prayer

There is nothing, in itself, surprising in the fact that we do not always 'get what we ask for' from God, our heavenly Father. The bowler prays for rain, and the batsman for fine weather; they cannot both be satisfied. The wisest and kindest human parents are not those who always give their children whatever they ask for.

But some Christians find it difficult to reconcile 'unanswered' prayer with some passages in the Gospels. Thus we read: 'Ask, and the gift will come, seek, and you shall find; knock, and the door shall be opened to you. Everyone that asks will receive, that seeks, will find, that knocks, will have the door opened to him' (Luke xi. 9f.). And again: 'You have only to make any request of the Father in my name, and he will grant it to you. Until now, you have not been making any requests in my name; make them, and they will be granted, to bring you gladness in full measure' (John xvi. 23f.).

The former of these passages need not, I think, detain us long. The rhythm of the words suggests poetry rather than matter-of-fact prose, and there is nothing to prove that particular favours are meant; the 'gift' in question may be the spiritual blessing of salvation.

The passage from St John's Gospel is rather different. It reads like prose, and indeed forms part of an intimate conversation between our Lord and the Twelve at the Last Supper. Part of the solution of the difficulty may lie in the twice repeated words 'in my name'. It may be that, here also, it is not a question of temporal favours but of the progress of the work which our Lord had come to do, and which he was now handing on to his disciples. As his devoted servants and friends, they would rejoice at the progress of that work, and they would pray for its progress. In general, then, our passage would contain an assurance that God would bless the progress of the Christian mission to mankind in response to the prayers of the missioners.

Even so, it may be objected that the prayers of individual Christians, and even the prayers of the Church at large, for the attainment of particular objectives within the general strategy of the campaign for the conversion of the world, often seem to go unanswered. We have been praying for years for the conversion of Russia. And as for the success of the campaign as a whole, what are we to make of the enigmatic saying: 'When the Son of Man comes, will he find faith left on the earth?' (Luke xviii. 8).

Perhaps the truth is, that we have to go a little deeper into the philosophy of prayer. Let it be granted that prayer 'in the name of Christ' is prayer for the accomplishment of the divine purpose incarnate in our Lord and his mission and redemptive work and passion. It is prayer, in other words, for the accomplishment of God's will 'in earth as it is in heaven'. But one thing is certain, that God's will is to us a mystery. What it is in the concrete we do not know; nor do we know what are the particular steps to its attainment. Hence, whenever we pray for some particular thing (like the conversion of Russia), we do so always with the implicit *proviso*: 'if such is in accordance with thy providential plan'. Though we ask for the conversion of Russia, we do not really *want* it unless it forms part of the divine plan, and even then only when and as it forms part of that plan.

Our prayer, in its deepest meaning of 'thy will be done', is one of the providential means of which God makes use for the accomplishment of his will. It is his good pleasure to make the accomplishment of his plan an answer to our prayers as well as a manifestation of his glory.

It may still be asked: Why then should we ever particularise our petitions? Why pray for the conversion of a friend, and not simply ask for the accomplishment of God's will?

It is probably true that, as we make progress in the spiritual life, there is a tendency towards some such simplification of our life of prayer. But it is also true that it is a good thing to retain *some* element of particular petitions. It seems more humble and child-like to do so. And it is probable that God actually inspires very holy people sometimes to make particular requests. For those of us who are still far from holiness, there is a danger that if we pray for nothing in particular we may almost unconsciously tend to give up praying altogether. And there is a danger that our life of particular desires may pursue its own course outside the ambit of our prayers, so that we shall be in some peril of becoming, spiritually, divided personalities. By praying for the things we superficially want, we consecrate our life of desire, and at the same time we tend to purify it and to develop the deepest desire of all, that God's will may in all things be perfectly accomplished.

iii

Corporate Prayer

The subject of this chapter, prayer in the worshipping community, is specially relevant to Catholic Christians. The chapter may be omitted by non-Christian readers without interrupting the sequence of the book as a whole.

The web of circumstance, in which each of us finds himself caught up as soon as he takes cognisance of his situation, includes other people. We are involved with other people in a multiplicity of ways. Each of us owes his existence to his parents, and most of us owe our upbringing and education to our childhood home. We are economically dependent on others, and human society provides the field in which we conduct our external life, the field in which the consequences of our internal decisions are worked out. Society has responsibilities towards us, and we have responsibilities towards society. To a very large extent, we are what society has made us; and society is what we all make of it. And once we have agreed to 'take God seriously', our obligations and responsibility to and for society take on a religious colour. In serving society, I am in the last resort serving God, and in serving God I am serving society.

Christianity presupposes this social aspect of human life. Not only has it taken over from Judaism the double precept: *Thou shalt love the Lord thy God . . . and thy neighbour as thyself;* but its central tenet only makes sense in a social context. The central affirmation of Christianity is that man's love for God is not an original spontaneity of man, but is a response by man to God's intervening love for man. This intervention of God took primary shape in an act of divine self-identification with man: in the Word of God, who is God, becoming man and redeeming us at a cost summed up in the crucifixion of the Word-made-man. Through this act of redemption man has been given the light for his understanding and the enablement for his will which, taken together, make it possible for each of us to live a life of right relationship with God — and therefore of right relationship with our total environment. In Christ, we are taught, each of us is to find the fullness of divine truth and grace; and without Christ 'we can do nothing' in the sphere of religion (John xv. 5).

Our salvation, then, the consequence of an act of God which in itself, in its inwardness, is one with the eternal act by which God is himself, is — from our point of view — wholly enshrined in, and can only flow from, a particular segment of total human history. It is enshrined in a complex of events which took place in Palestine nearly two thousand years ago: 'he has been revealed once for all, at the moment when history reached its fulfilment, annulling our sin by his sacrifice' (Hebrews ix. 26).

How is a man, living thousands of miles and thousands of years away from this particular segment of history, to make contact with the complex of saving events? How does the truth of them come to him, and how is the grace they contain transmitted? How does the Christ of first-century Palestine become contemporary with the European, the Asian, the African, of today?

The answer is: by the mediation of the Church, the Church which is 'his body, the completion of him who everywhere and in all things is complete' (Ephesians i. 23).

In becoming man, the Word of God accepted the particularity of human conditions which is the lot of every man. He was born into, and grew up in, a particular social religious tradition, the tradition which is disclosed to us in the pages of the Old Testament and is presupposed by the New. His mission from his heavenly Father was to all people in all ages. But it took shape in the first instance in a mission to his own people, as an invitation and a challenge to that people to recognise in him the embodied fulfilment of their religious hopes and ideals. He was that people, Israel, personified and epitomised; and henceforward the criterion of the true Israelite was to surrender to the truth and the implications of this claim.

'He came to what was his own, and they who were his own gave him no welcome' (John i. 11). The Gospel story is of a mission that 'failed' —failed to the point of his being handed over by the religious leaders of his people to the secular arm of Rome and to the Roman punishment of crucifixion. But there were some, a 'little flock', who did surrender to his claim, and these became the nucleus of the renovated Israel, the Church.

To this society, which was continuous with the Old

Testament People of God, yet profoundly transformed by its faith in Jesus as the Christ, he bequeathed the extension of his own mission: 'I came upon an errand from my Father, and now I am sending you out in my turn' (John xx. 21). This society was to speak in his name; his teaching was to be its teaching, its teaching his. Thus it was to "present" him in his aspect of divine truth revealed to men. And sacramentally he bequeathed to it also his Body and his Blood, the very life of that grace which he had won for men in the sacrifice of the Cross. So, through this society, man everywhere and at all times was to receive the divine help, the grace, which is God's love for men in intervening action. The sacrament of baptism, by which this grace is initially given to each of us, is at the same time the outward rite by which we are incorporated into, become members of, the society; members of this 'body of Christ'. And the Eucharistic prayer-sacrament-sacrifice is at once the means by which the baptismal life of each of us is fed and deepened, and the rite by which we grow more deeply into the implications of our membership of the society. The Eucharist is the sacrament of our unity with God, and identically the sacrament of our unity with our fellow-believers.

The Church is the divinely intended and achieved religious incorporation of humanity. Its vocation has two aspects, like the vocation of its Founder, of which indeed it is an extension. Jesus Christ was at once God's envoy to mankind and the personification of man's response to the divine invitation. He was the true human worshipper 'in spirit and in truth' (John iv. 23). The sacrifice of the Cross was at once God's supreme appeal to man and man's supreme act of prayer and adoration. So too the Church is at once the vehicle of God's grace and truth to us, and also the incorporation of man's answering worship.

At the same time, the Church is an actual human society. As such, it leads an actual corporate life, and its worship includes corporate acts of worship, of which the central and highest act is the Eucharistic celebration, what we Western Catholics call the Mass.

Since the Church is our link with Christ and with God in Christ, it is obvious that each of us is called upon to take a share in the Eucharistic celebration. We do so by attending Mass and co-operating, by our intention, with the offering of the Mass-sacrifice by the priest and the congregation. We do so still more perfectly when our attendance at Mass culminates in Holy Communion.

How often? The Church herself tells us what she regards as a minimum. Unless reasonably prevented, we are to attend Mass on Sundays and the holy days 'of obligation'; and to receive Holy Communion once a year, during the period of the 'Easter precept'. By obedience to these requirements we exercise our right and duty as members of the body of Christ.

Catholics who read these pages are not likely to need instructions on the mode of preparation for Holy Communion, on the dispositions with which this sacrament should be received, and on the thanksgiving which is appropriate after reception. But a few words on attendance at Mass and on 'praying the Mass' may not be out of place.

Since we are bound to attend Mass on Sundays and holy days of obligation, it may be remarked here that we fulfil this obligation if we are actually present and awake at Mass, not by mere accident or external constraint, but with the intention of being present and praying; and one's attention should be such that one is aware of the progress of the Mass or of its principal parts.

But if we think of Mass attendance as a privilege and not only as a duty, then we may well wish to make the most of our attendance as an act of prayer. We are present not just as solitary individuals but as members of the praying Church. The Mass is a corporate act, and we normally express our co-operation in a corporate act by external gesture and utterance. Thus in a meeting of a committee of which we are a member, even if we do not contribute to the discussions we express our vote by word or action.

Similarly, we can show our co-operation with the corporate act which is the Mass by joining in the outward acts of the congregation. We can kneel when the congregation kneels, stand or sit when it stands or sits. And if, as is often the case today, the Mass is sung, or is a 'dialogue Mass', we can take part in the singing or in the 'dialogue'. Such external co-operation helps to deepen the congregation's sense of being engaged in a common task, and it is of psychological value to each individual. It 'takes us out of ourselves', to use a hackneyed expression, and this is not unimportant for our spiritual life.

On the other hand, there is some danger of exaggeration in the modern tendency to stress the value of external co-operation with the Mass. The Church herself is coming to emphasise this value more and more. But we must distinguish between what the Church prescribes and what she only encourages. As we have seen, what she prescribes as an obligatory minimum, and so far as is necessary to obey our *obligation* of Mass attendance, is very restricted indeed.

Again, it seems legitimate to distinguish between attendance at Mass which is obligatory, and attending Masses which
are not 'of obligation'. The Church's encouragement to co-
operate externally in the way we have described may be taken
as referring primarily to our behaviour at Mass when attendance is obligatory, because it is these Masses which are the
primary expression of our will to participate in the corporate
worship of the Church. But many devout Catholics attend a
certain number of Masses beyond the bare minimum prescribed; some go to Mass almost every day. These same persons
may wish to say the Rosary daily, or to make a daily meditation or mental prayer. Time is limited, and it may not be
feasible to keep up these practices and also go to Mass (we are
not speaking of obligatory Mass) —unless the Rosary is said or
the meditation made during Mass. In such cases, and in others,
it is surely obvious that to insist on 'external participation' is to
present the person in question with a choice that he should
not have to make. To do one's mental prayer in the quiet
circumstances of a low Mass may be better than either to omit
the mental prayer or to omit the Mass.

Like the Mass, baptism is a corporate act of the Church; no
less an act than the solemn admission of a new member. The
new liturgy for the Easter Vigil reminds us that in ancient
times catechumens were solemnly baptised at the Easter Mass
in the presence of the body of the faithful. Such can hardly be
the usual custom in modern Christian lands, where baptism is
usually administered very shortly after birth. The saving up of
an adult convert for baptism at the Easter Vigil may well
constitute a real spiritual hardship for him, and in any case the
practice today would lack some of the realism of the ancient
usage, though in suitable circumstances it is recommended by

authority. But it would be an excellent thing if not only the family of an infant but the local congregation were more frequently encouraged to attend its baptism, thus emphasising the importance to the society, which is the Church, of the admission of a new member.

In fact, every sacrament is an act of the Church and so has a 'corporate aspect'. It is true that the Church has long ago, and very wisely, given up the practice of public penance, and insists with the strongest possible seriousness on the complete secrecy of sacramental confession. But the priest in the confessional, despite the secrecy surrounding his ministrations, is at one and the same time the representative of Christ and of the Church.

Sacramental confession is necessary and obligatory only for the forgiveness of grave sin committed after baptism (strictly speaking, even the normal obligation of seeking and gaining absolution 'at least once a year' only holds for those who have committed a mortal sin since their last confession-and-absolution). But grave sin on the part of a baptised person is not only an offence against God but an offence against the Church, since the soul of the Church, its interior spiritual bond, is sanctifying grace (which is incompatible with grave sin). Sacramental absolution is thus a reconciliation with the Church as well as with God. Indeed, there is good authority for the view that 'the meaning of the words of absolution is first of all a reconciliation with the Church' and that it is *as* a reconciliation with the Church that absolution is efficacious of reconciliation with God.[1]

---

[1] Bernard Leeming, *Principles of Sacramental Theology*, p. 361

The liturgy of the Mass and the other sacramental rites are divinely instituted factors in the prayer-life of the Church. But the Church prays corporately in other ways too. The Breviary Offices (Matins, Lauds, etc.) are by their original nature modes of corporate worship. They are of obligation for priests and for many religious Orders and are of course adaptable for the laity also. For most priests they have become a form of private prayer, but it is private prayer of a special kind, inasmuch as it is prescribed by the Church and its performance unites us in a special way with the corporate prayer of the Church.

Besides the Breviary, mention may be made here of Benediction, the Stations of the Cross (which may also be done as a private devotion), parochial missions, and retreats and pilgrimages. The life of the parish (the natural community unit of the Church) is expressed in such ways, and a good Catholic will normally recognise the privilege of taking part in them according to his circumstances and his own spiritual needs; and he will recognise that by so doing he contributes to the corporate spiritual vitality of the parish. At the same time, he will make a clear distinction between matters of obligation, like attendance at Mass on Sundays and holy days of obligation, and other practices which are laudable in themselves but whose adoption is left to his discretion.

The modern 'liturgical movement' is one of the most hopeful signs of Catholic revival and adaptation. It is profoundly in harmony with the genius of Christianity which, as it were, consecrates the fact of man's social nature, reminding us that as we owe our natural birth and well-being to others, so also we owe our supernatural birth and spiritual well-being to the society which Christ instituted and in which he 'prolongs' his own life and work. But like all good things, the movement is liable to give occasion to exaggeration and abuse. It is well to remind ourselves that society has no life apart from the life of its members, the human beings who compose it. The heart of human life is the life of our intellect and will, and the intellectual, volitional life is rooted in the mystery of our incommunicable personalities. There is a sense in which each of us lives for society and in which society has rights over us which we must not seek to evade. In an even deeper sense, society exists for the sake of the incommunicable personal life of its members.

What is true of natural society is true, in due proportion, of the Christian society, the Church. Just as, according to an old adage, the sacraments are 'for the sake of men' (and not men for the sake of the sacraments), so too the Church, which can be described as a sacramental society, is 'for the sake of its members'. The whole ministry of grace and truth is directed to the birth and progress of that life of supernatural friendship with God which is called 'sanctifying grace'; and sanctifying grace is a quality of the incommunicable spirit of a person and has its first expression in acts of faith, hope and charity which are acts of man's interior intellect and will. We must not emphasise corporate prayer to a degree in which it tends to stifle the impulse of private prayer and interior spiritual communion with God for which we were made, which is to be our heritage in heaven, and which is anticipated on earth in the 'mystical' life of the soul tending through and beyond all created things to God himself in his triune life. It is this interior life of the human spirit which is the very soul, not only of the Church considered as a society of human beings, but of the sacraments which the Church dispenses. It is quite true that the sacraments confer grace *ex opere operato*, and that in particular 'the unworthiness of the minister hindereth not the effect of a sacrament'. But there is one interior act of the minister which is essential to the validity of a sacrament: his intention to perform the sacramental rite; if a priest says the words of consecration at Mass but has no intention of consecrating, there is no consecration. Similarly, as we have seen, the obligation of attending Mass is not fulfilled by mere physical presence in the place where Mass is celebrated; there is further required an intention of being present and even some minimum of attention to what is going on. Thus the heart of corporate prayer is the incommunicable prayer of the individual.

iv

The Adventure of Prayer

Prayer is our freely willed response to the fact of our utter dependence, and the utter dependence of the whole created universe, on God. God is the one answer to everything that is implied in all the questionings of our intellect, the answer which alone saves our situation from intolerable absurdity. He is the absolutely satisfying lodestar of our desire for the good; and all desire is for 'the good'. He is the reality of all value, all worth-whileness. He is the source of the relative reality and relative worth of all created things and persons; the source of their reality and the source of their activity. He is thus the Lord of history. Prayer is the acknowledgement of God and our relation to him, in adoration and thanksgiving, in penitence and petition. It is the activity, then, in which we 'react' and 'adapt ourselves' to God, our ultimate environment; in which therefore we first become fully ourselves, first exploit the deepest potentialities of our created, spiritual, nature.

In our second chapter we argued that we ought to have a rule of prayer, as a safeguard against our natural instability and negligence. If we have no rule of prayer, it is not likely that prayer will become the pervading reality of our interior life that it ought to be. By conforming to a rule we develop a habit. And with the help of a habit we do easily and frequently what otherwise requires a whole series of separate and difficult efforts. Thus, during the second world war, the rules of rationing in Britain developed a habit of feeding which, unpleasant though it was, was relatively easy; it became, as we say, 'second nature' to us, and if we had suddenly returned to pre-war meals our nature would have felt the shock.

But prayer is something more than mere regularity, just as poetry is something more than mere conformity with metrical rules. If we are content with mere regularity in our spiritual life, we may easily fall into formalism. You can go on kissing your wife good-bye in the morning long after love has died from your heart, and it is not likely that she is deceived by the formal gesture.

Prayer is more than the reciting of some prescribed forms at fixed times. It is the 'lifting up of the mind and heart' to God. Outward forms, without the interior spirit, are like a body from which the soul has fled, and God, who is the 'searcher of the heart', is not deceived. Prayer is our life of personal intercourse or communion with God, who loves us, and whom we love or want to love. Love will not be satisfied with rules; it may recognise their value and obey them, but it will always go beyond them in creative personal spontaneity.

A young lover will often think of his absent friend; his thought is drawn to his friend as the compass needle seems to be drawn to the magnetic north, or as water seems to be drawn to find its own level. His memory and imagination combine to recall the well-known features and the accents of the familiar voice. He relives and ponders over past conversations. He reads and re-reads, and 'reads between the lines of', his friend's letters. He cherishes and studies his portrait. He forgets his immediate surroundings and is 'lost to the world', as he dwells in thought where his beloved is.

The object of desire is the good. God is the absolute and transcendent Good, and religion is the expression of our deepest, all-inclusive, desire. There are no words that can adequately represent the depth of this desire, but religion is not afraid to use natural analogies: 'O God, my whole soul longs for thee, as a deer for running water; my whole soul thirsts for God, the living God; shall I never again make my pilgrimage into God's presence?'[1]

If it is proper to compare our desire for God with the thirst of a deer for running water, it is proper to compare it with the love of a human being for a fellow-human, and Christianity has not hesitated to read into the Canticle of Canticles an allegory of divine love:

> My true love, I am all his; and who but I the longing of his heart? . . . Hold me close to thy heart, close as locket or bracelet fits; not death itself is so strong as love, not the grave itself so cruel as love unrequited; the torch that lights it is a blaze of fire. Yes, love is a fire no waters avail to quench, no floods to drown;

[1] Psalm xli. 2f.

for love, a man will give up all that he has in the world, and think nothing of his loss.[2]

As we remember, imagine, and think about an absent friend, so it is right that we should ponder prayerfully about God.[3] If we love God, or if we only want to love God (and to want to love him is the essence of loving him), it is surely not unnatural that we should take the trouble to think about him, to ponder over his greatness and his goodness, his power and wisdom, his mercy towards us, and the fact that our desire to love him is the effect and the proof of his love for us, which forever precedes and creates our love for him.

There is, of course, a difficulty. God, in the mystery of his transcendent Godhead, is inconceivable and unimaginable. For all his nearness, he is eternally beyond the furthest reach of our questing minds. 'No man has ever seen God'.[4] His thoughts are not as our thoughts, nor his ways as our ways. The gulf between our creaturehood and his infinity is itself infinite. To invite a man to 'think about God' is, it will be argued, as though one should invite a pet dog to appreciate the differential calculus or the beauty of great music.

But still the desire for God is there, built into our nature and ineluctable. And the gulf which no human initiative can

---

[2] Canticle of Canticles, vii. 10, viii. 6f.

[3] There is a traditional name for such 'prayerful pondering'. It is called meditation. I have not used this word in the text above, because it may sound strange, even forbidding. It is too easy to suppose that meditation is something for very holy people, or at least for 'professional' religious people like monks or nuns. But if we forget the word and think of the reality for which it stands, meditation (or 'prayerful pondering') is something very simple, even obvious; something obviously appropriate for everyone who recognises that to love God is his supreme duty and privilege.

[4] John i. 18

bridge is bridged, so Christians believe, by revelation; an infinite gulf, spanned by the infinite power and wisdom and goodness of the infinite God.

God has revealed himself to us not only in the remote way of the footprints of his power upon creation, but personally as Jesus Christ, who is not only truly God but truly man, someone we can both imagine and think about, and even sympathise with; someone whom the Church 'remembers'. No man has ever seen God. But 'Whoever has seen me, has seen the Father'.[5]

So we can 'prayerfully ponder' about God by picturing to ourselves the scenes and events of our Lord's life, and we can, in imagination, listen to his teaching in the Gospels. We can place ourselves among the crowd that hung on his words as he taught from the boat on the sea of Galilee: 'Then he began to teach by the seaside again; and a great multitude gathered before him, so that he went into a boat, and sat there on the sea, while all the multitude was on the land, at the sea's edge. And he taught them for a long time, but in parables.' We can reconstruct the setting of this teaching, so humble and so idyllic: the little boat moving slightly with the blue water of the lake, the crowd in a semi-circle under the already brilliant morning sun of a Palestinian springtime, when 'almost suddenly' the blood-red anemone, the gay tulip, the spotless narcissus, and the golden ranunculus clothe the fields, the fields 'already rich with the promise of a harvest to be gathered in due time'.[6] Thus we can dispose ourselves with the crowd to listen to the word of him who spoke as 'nobody had ever

---

[5] John xiv. 9.
[6] Edersheim, *Jesus the Messiah*, abridged edition, pp. 165f.

spoken' (John vii. 46): 'A sower went out to sow . . .'[7] And as we listen we can apply the parable to ourselves. The 'good soil', we are told by St Luke (viii. 15), stands for those who 'hear the word, and hold by it with a noble and generous heart, and endure'; in these it grew and yielded abundant harvest for the Sower. God, then, asks from me a 'noble and generous', or, as another translation has it, an 'honest and good' heart. It is God himself, made man for my salvation, who speaks these words. And he addresses them to me personally, just as if I had actually been there by the lakeside, listening. He speaks to me with infinite wisdom, and in infinite mercy. His limitless power, then, will do all in me, if I oppose no resistance to his call and grace; if I present him, on my side, with an 'honest and good heart'. And I shall not forget that he who gives grace, the seed of glory, will give me, if I am not unwilling, this honest and good heart to receive and respond to the grace. I may remind myself that merely to recognise the existence of God may make sense of my 'situation', but it does not automatically correct what is warped in my attitude and reaction to the situation. I need not only God's truth but his 'grace' if my attitude is to be correct and healthy. If I am to be healed, it is God in Christ who must heal me (Jeremias xvii. 14).

When we have been remembering, imagining, and thinking about an absent friend, we say to ourselves: 'If only he were here now, so that I could speak to him face to face, tell him of my love again, and hear him tell me of his love for me.' *Yet seem'd it winter still, and you away.*

Here, however, our comparison of things human and divine breaks down magnificently. God, free from the limita-

---

[7]Mark iv. 1-3.

tions of time as from every other limitation, is present everywhere and at all times. He is present now, more intimately
present to my situation and to me than I am present to myself,
more lovingly, in Christ, concerned with me than I have ever
been concerned with him. So, from our imagining and thinking about God revealed in Jesus Christ, we go on quite
normally — as it were with a sigh of enraptured relief — to
direct 'speaking' to him, whether in words, spoken or thought,
or in wordless interior acts of adoration, love, thanksgiving,
petition. Thus our 'pondering' has melted into 'prayer'. It is
informal, spontaneous, intimate, adventurous, prayer. Heart
speaks to heart. A lover does not need to prepare formal
addresses of welcome and flattery to welcome the beloved.
And in fact, love needs very few words.

What shall we 'say' to God in our prayer? We can pray to
him about the things suggested by our pondering. Thus, if our
subject of thought has been the parable by the lakeside, we can
acknowledge what dead and worthless spiritual 'soil' we are
unless he, the Sower, gives his divine seed. We can thank him
for having taken pity on our extreme need by sowing this seed
in his incarnate life, and at the cost to himself of Calvary. We
can deplore and in intention renounce 'the cares of this world
and the deceitfulness of riches and the other appetites' (Mark
iv. 19) which, so far, have smothered the seed of the divine
word in us, 'so that it remains fruitless'. We can ask him, as we
have so often asked him, for help and rescue from ourselves:
'Master my rebellious will.'

But of course we need not confine our prayer to thoughts
directly suggested by our previous 'pondering'. If we have any
pressing cares or worries, any special joys or hopes, we can
speak to him about them. Whatever interests us is of interest

to him, however trivial. We are encouraged to see ourselves as 'children' of our heavenly Father. When a schoolboy comes home from school, he pours out all his new interests to his mother or father, and the parent is happy to listen.

We do well, during these periods of pondering and prayer, to pause sometimes, as though to allow opportunity for God, in his turn, to 'speak' to us. Not that we should expect or desire anything miraculous like the 'voices' of St Joan of Arc. Not, again, that we should foolishly mistake our own bright ideas for divine inspirations. All the same, it is good to rest from time to time in God's presence, remembering that we are incapable, apart from grace, of fashioning any salutary thoughts or shaping any acceptable prayers. 'We do not know what prayer to offer, to pray as we ought', but we can give the Holy Spirit scope to pray within us 'with groans beyond all utterance' (or, as we may translate the phrase, 'with yearnings that cannot be formulated in words') (Romans viii. 26).

Although we have spoken of 'going on' from pondering to direct prayer, it is probable that many people will in practice find that it is easy, and more satisfactory, to interweave their prayer with their 'pondering', and *vice versa*. When we are thinking or imagining, we are doing this as in God's presence, and when we pray to him, it is to the One who reveals himself in the sayings and events of the Gospel about which we have been thinking.

We can expect that the practice of prayer and of thinking about God and his revelation will make us more conscious of the disharmony between our life and the ideals which move us to pray. We may be tempted to feel that our prayer is not 'genuine' because our life is in such disaccord with it. But what we have to realise is that, in fact, it is our *life* which is not genuine, because it does not correspond with what we believe to be true. Our aim, then, will be to 'integrate' the rest of our life with our prayer. For many people, it is a salutary practice to take away from their prayer not only a general intention to reform their life but some practical and particular decision apt for the expected circumstances of the day that lies before them: an act of kindness to be performed, an occasion of ill-temper to be avoided or, if unavoidable, to be surmounted.

Our decision, whether a general one or whether both general and particular, can become the subject of our concluding petitions to God, that he would bless it and give us the grace to be faithful to it.

It is obvious enough that the 'prayerful pondering' which has been the subject of the present chapter is something essentially quite 'normal'. It involves no pretensions to special expertise, or to special holiness. If we admit that we are very 'average' people, very poor specimens of humanity, then the sincere thing is, to want to improve. What better way to seek improvement than to seek, by dwelling on God and his revelation, to make God and his love more 'real' to ourselves; and then to pray to him and to ask his grace to amend our lives? The question is not, therefore, whether we are good enough to take up the practice of 'prayerful pondering' but whether we are good enough to be able to do without it.

The kind of prayer we have here been considering is one that does not fall under strict rules, inasmuch as it is directed towards an informal intercourse with God. Yet it is a good thing to have a rule concerned with it. It is an excellent thing so to arrange your life that there may be a daily period of time set apart for this kind of prayer. The length of this period will vary from case to case, as will the time of day chosen for it. For some the morning will be the most practicable choice and the most fruitful time; for others it may be the evening. If one can devote a daily half-hour to the practice, that is an admirable thing. The lives of very many today, however, are so busy that it may be difficult to reserve more than a quarter of an hour, or even ten minutes, to 'prayerful pondering'. The important thing, as with morning and evening prayers, is to have a rule and to be faithful to it despite all discouragements, of which there will be many.

Some may be helped by one or other of various books which give pattern meditations, such as Challoner's or Bede Jarrett's. Certainly a book of that kind is a useful introduction to unfamiliar country. If one does not follow a book, it is a good thing to have some sort of scheme for subjects of 'pondering'. For instance, one could take one of the Gospels and go through it paragraph by paragraph, one paragraph each day (missing out, of course, passages which suggest no helpful thoughts to one, e.g. the genealogy in St Matthew ch. i). One could vary this scheme on feast days by choosing a passage from the Gospel of the day. Obviously, too, one could use an Epistle instead of a Gospel. In any case, the aim is not so much to do some Bible reading as to do some 'thinking' —about the Friend who is never absent.

Prayer is an adventure into the unplumbed depths of the love of God, the depths of God who is love. It is a highly personal activity, and is as various as the variety of human temperaments and the stages of individual development. We must be ready to experiment in prayer, to find 'by trial and error' the way that seems suited to us. We are, it has been said, to 'pray as we can, and not to try to pray as we can't'. And having found a way of prayer which 'works' for us, we must still be ready to move on to a new way, or another stage, when our needs change. But deeper than our quest of God there is God's quest of us. Since he wants us to pray, we can and should believe that, if we will do our part with the help of his grace, he will lead us into the paths of prayer that he wishes us to follow. Hence we must always be ready to surrender our own spiritual preference and devices, and to let him substitute for them the sort of prayer that he chooses for us.

V

Prayer and Life

There used to be a fashion of equating religion with magic, or at least of suggesting that religion derives from magic. It may sometimes be difficult to draw the line between behaviour which is inspired by religious motives and behaviour which is basically magical. And it is possible, if not probable, that some human behaviour is partly religious and partly magical in its motivation. In idea, however, the two things are quite distinct. Magic, according to the dictionary, is 'the pretended art of influencing the course of events by occult control of nature or of spirits'.[1] The word in this definition which distinguishes magic from religious prayer is 'control'. Magic, in other words, is basically an attempt to subject the will 'of nature or of spirits', or it may be of God himself, to the will of man. Religion, fundamentally, is the attempt to subject the will of man to the will of God.

[1] *Concise Oxford Dictionary, s.v.*

Prayer is a religious activity. Even petitionary prayer for temporal benefits is, in essence, not an attempt to force God's hand, but an appeal to his good pleasure. It recognises God as the source of all good, and as himself the supreme Good. If it is humble and thoughtful prayer, it concedes that we may be mistaken in specifying the object of some particular desire as being really conducive to our long-term happiness. The humble believer prays, as Christ prayed, with the at least implicit proviso: 'Thy will be done.'

The believer is in no doubt that what is according to the will of God will ultimately be conducive to his own welfare and happiness.   But the believer who loves God, while acknowledging this material identity of God's will and glory and his own highest ends, is more concerned for the fulfilment of God's will because it *is* God's will, and for the glory of God, than he is for his own happiness. After all, God (and God's will, which is identical with God) is the 'supreme value'. If it is possible to make a rational distinction where there is no distinction in objective fact, it is rational to say that the realisation of what God wills is far more important in the total scheme of things than the realisation of my own happiness. The lover of God 'prefers' the God of Paradise to the Paradise of God. It is the ambition of love to purify itself of all selfish taint and to exult in the paradox: 'I should be happy in the happiness of the Beloved, even if that happiness could only be attained by my unhappiness.'

For all of us except our Lord and his Mother, our prayer-life is not the whole, but a part, of our total life. But it is really a part. It is the same person who at one moment is praying and, at another, managing his business, doing the housework, or quarreling over a game of cards. And each of us is a developing personality, tending (let us hope) towards an integration of his multiple activities under the aegis of a dominant and unifying purpose.

There is thus an intimate relationship between our life of prayer and the rest of our life. It is psychologically very difficult to be spending the major part of our life in a deliberate pursuit of aims which we recognise to be contrary to the will of God, and yet to be leading a serious life of prayer inspired by the *leit-motiv*: 'Not my will but thine be done.' In the measure that such prayer is genuine, it demands to exert its influence on the rest of our life and to bring our actions into closer harmony with itself. In our previous chapter we were considering a kind of prayer which aims at a high degree of this 'genuineness'. It is also a kind of prayer which tends to lead to major developments in the prayer-life of the person who regularly practises it. We shall expect that, as our spiritual life as a whole progresses, as we become in the ordinary walks of life more truly (though with no priggishness) 'people of God', there will be progress in our prayer-life. And from the opposite point of view, we may hope that as our prayer-life develops, the rest of our life will tend to be reformed. Prayer, the catechism teaches, is an 'ordinary means of grace'.

The first step in actual friendship with God is taken when a person decides to exclude from his voluntary life whatever is strictly incompatible with such friendship (a Catholic calls this the purpose of eschewing 'grave' or 'mortal' sin).[2] We are

---

[2] For many persons, baptised in infancy and well brought up in a good Catholic home, this 'decision' will have been coincident with the dawn of reason. As it will have been entirely in line with the grace given to them in baptism, and in harmony with the atmosphere of the home and the habits inculcated by instruction and example, it will probably have left no trace on their conscious memory.

encouraged to compare our relations to God with those of a child to a wise and loving father. It is obvious that a father will make small account of the trivial faults of a child who really loves him but is only slowly learning to control his passions. It is also obvious that the father's attitude will be different if the child deliberately and in a serious matter defies his father's will and command. Such behaviour, until repentance intervenes, clearly throws the child out of due relation to its father; not because the father's love for it has ceased, but because the child's will is no longer directed towards real 'friendship' with its father. Repentance, in reference to man as the creature and child of God, means that with one's will one renounces whatever makes real friendship with God impossible, so far as it makes it impossible.

It should be noticed that we have spoken of a 'decision' to eschew grave sin. This, as experience and common sense teach, does not in all cases mean that we shall never in fact commit grave sin. 'The best-laid schemes o' mice and men gang aft a-gley.' If, despite our previous resolution, we have the misfortune to commit serious sin and thus to break our resolution, our task (with God's help) will be to 'repent' and renew our good resolution. When the resolution has been taken, and so long as it is not broken, we are in a state of friendship with God, the normal presupposition for the serious development of our life of prayer.[3]

This decision or resolution, which is within the power of each of us by the help of the grace that God will certainly not

---

[3]It must not be thought that until the above decision has been taken all prayer is impossible. A person who has not yet made the decision needs above all to pray for grace to do so; there is no graver need than this between the cradle and the grave. And of course his prayer need not be restricted either to this petition or to petitions in general. He can and should adore God, and thank him for his mercies and favours.

withhold, may be called a first 'conversion' or 'turning'. Like St Paul's Thessalonian converts, one who has made the resolution has 'turned away' from the idolatry of aims which are incompatible with God 'to serve a living God, a God who really exists' (1 Thessalonians i. 9).

As has been said, it is a first step in the actual love of God, but it is not meant to be the last. A second step will soon be suggested by our prayer itself, and grace will enable us to renounce, in intention, not only everything that is strictly incompatible with the divine friendship, but all deliberate and voluntary clinging to minor indulgences such as are too trivial to 'break' our state of friendship with God yet plainly, so far as they spring from deliberate and habitual purpose, do reduce our friendship for him to a somewhat heavily qualified one. We spoke in the second chapter of one such indulgence: failing to get up punctually in the morning. Many others will suggest themselves to the mind of anyone who is accustomed to take note of his own behaviour: minor extravagance in the use of money, irritability, over-preoccupation with the pleasures of the table, various kinds of selfishness and inconsiderateness in our relations with others . . . A person who is faithfully and regularly practising the kind of prayer outlined in the previous chapter, and especially a Catholic who is a frequent communicant, will both see the desirability of renouncing such indulgences (in intention) and will also receive the grace to make such a renunciation.

Once again, however, it is to be observed that it is one thing to make a resolution by which one renounces deliberate voluntary attachment to such 'venial' sins; it is quite another thing in fact never to fall into such sins. The battle against temptation may be life-long, and we can expect to be 'wounded' in the course of it. The great thing is not to be discouraged by such falls, and above all not to suppose for a moment that, because of them, we 'may as well' give up our prayer-life. On the contrary, they should be an added incentive to prayer, since through prayer we may hope to obtain the grace we need for the battle of life. *God knoweth whereof we are made.* It has often been remarked that even great saints have not all conquered some human weakness, for instance impatience of temper; and it is usually added that God presumably has left them with these weaknesses in order to preserve and deepen their humility. It is certainly true that complacency about one's spiritual achievement and progress is profoundly out of harmony with the spirit of prayer. As prayer deepens in us a realisation of the holiness of God, it makes us more acutely conscious of the contrast between it and our spiritual misery. Thus saints grow in humility as they grow in the other virtues. But humility must be joined to a limitless trust in God's goodness, his love for us, the power of his grace.

There is still a further step to be taken in the adaptation of our life in general to the implications of our prayer-life. Or rather it is not a step but a stage with unlimited progressive degrees. It is characterised throughout by one basic purpose, decision, or resolution: to aim, so far as in one lies, with the help of the grace God bestows, at the perfection of the love of God. It is what a celebrated spiritual writer of the eighteenth century, Grou, calls 'devotion': 'that disposition . . . which is ready to do everything and to suffer everything' for God. And he repeats: 'True and solid devotion is that disposition of the heart by which we are ready to do and to suffer, without exception or reserve, everything which comes from God's good pleasure, everything which is the will of God.'[4]

Grou's use of the word 'devotion' in this context calls for some comment. There is a tendency for money to decline in real value: the debasement of the currency. There is a similar tendency in language. The word 'devotion' today often suggests a kind of sentimental pietism (having a 'warm feeling' towards God and an attraction for religious services and practices comparable to the attraction some people feel for television or surf-bathing). Grou, of course, means nothing of the sort. He was a classical scholar and was presumably aware that in Latin 'to devote oneself' meant to sacrifice one's life, e.g. for the safety of the fatherland: Livy speaks of men 'rushing upon the enemy with devoted bodies' — throwing their lives away like the men of the Light Brigade. So Grou's 'devotion' is something not essentially emotional or sentimental at all, but a total self-committal to God to the exclusion of all rival claims and interests, a self-committal springing not from the emotions but the will, and justified not by sentiment but by a cool intellectual appraisal of God's rights over us.

The logic behind such a dispostion of 'devotion' is incontrovertible. God is the supreme value, the creator, the Lord of history. He can only have made us for himself. He obviously cannot have any legitimate rival; he is what may be called 'the incomparable good'. Being made for him, and called by him, we ought to seek, and can obviously find, no satisfaction, in the long run, outside of him; and any pursuit which does not lead us towards a closer and fuller union with him is manifestly a futile distraction from our real end. The 'devout' person is one who can give a religious twist to the words of the

[4]Grou, *Manual for Interior Souls*, p. 1.

poet, whenever some created object offers itself as a substitute
for closer union with God:

> I could not love thee, dear, so much
>   Lov'd I not honour more—

or to that other poet's description of the Happy Warrior:

> 'Tis, finally, the Man, who, lifted high,
> Conspicuous object in a nation's eye,
> Or left unthought-of in obscurity, —
> Who, with a toward or untoward lot,
> Prosperous or adverse, to his wish or not —
> *Plays, in the many games of life, that one*
> *Where what he most doth value must be won:*
> Whom neither shape of danger can dismay,
> Nor thought of tender happiness betray;
> Who, not content that former worth stand fast,
> Looks forward, persevering to the last,
> From well to better, daily self-surpast.

The logic of devotion can be appreciated by any of us. But
to have the disposition of devotion it is necessary to have
chosen the path of devotion by an act of our will. We may
'find ourselves' disposed to optimism or pessimism, to external
activity or to contemplation. But devotion, being a habit of the
will, springs from an interior act of deliberate choice. Once
again, we are dealing with a 'conversion', comparable to the
first conversion by which we decided to eschew grave offence
against God from our lives.

In his remarkable and most moving book, *The Lost World of
the Kalahari*, Colonel Laurens van der Post tells how he once

wrote, in a diary of his boyhood: 'I have decided today that when I am grown-up I am going into the Kalahari Desert to seek out the Bushman.' He goes on to describe how, in the years that followed, this resolution became 'obscured'; how circumstances many years later revived the powerful interest that had dominated his childhood; and how he 'tried to persuade more fully qualified people, scientists, anthropologists and psychologists to follow up this line of living research', but in vain, and so:

> I found myself compelled against my conscious will towards the conclusion that, ridiculous as it might seem, I myself ought perhaps to take up the spoor where it vanished in the sand. Then one morning I awoke to find that, in sleep, my mind had been decided for me. 'I will go and find the Bushman,' I told myself, suddenly amazed that so simple a statement had never presented itself to me before. . . .
>
> Throughout the ages life appeared to build up great invisible charges like clouds and earth of electricity, until suddenly in a sultry hour the spirit moved, the wind rose, a drop of rain fell acid in the dust, fire flared in the nerve, and drums rolled to produce what we call thunder and lightning in the heavens, and chance and change in human society and personality.
>
> Something of this sort, in a small way, had happened to me overnight. I, who had been going round in circles for twenty long years in the particular matter of the Bushman, had now not only found my way but wanted to go at once.[5]

The sensitive reader will find many points of interest in these revealing sentences. There is the 'compulsion against the

---

[5] *The Lost World of the Kalahari* (Hogarth Press, 1958), pp. 60, 67-9.

conscious will', the gradual sense of being cornered by a destiny which one has not chosen, and for which nevertheless one has been disposing oneself for years. There is the protest of conventional reason: '*ridiculous* as it might seem.' There is the movement of recoil or evasion in 'perhaps'; and yet there is the old, now glowing, vision of the goal: 'to take up the spoor.' And then there is the complete simplicity and obviousness of the decision once it has been taken. A revolution, a 'conversion', has taken place in that innermost hold of the spirit from which the creative acts of human history spring forth; and the world will never again be the same for the person who has experienced the revolution, or for the human society in which he lives. Observe, too, how (as so often in the history of holy people) the child has played out in anticipation an act of the spirit which yet only became real when the mature person rediscovered his childish inspiration and endorsed it: 'I have decided today that *when I am grown-up ...*'; and then, 'I will go and find the Bushman.'

On one point one would wish for a slight clarification: 'I awoke to find that, in sleep, *my mind had been decided for me.*' But in fact, a person's mind is never 'decided for him' without his consenting to the decision; and this consent is his own act, hardly done in sleep. No one has the right to pronounce on the inner life of anyone else; still, I would suggest that what probably happened to Colonel Van der Post was that the final adjustments of his nerve centres were taking place in sleep, and that, on waking, his spirit, which had been long moving towards the fateful decision, found now no interior obstacles to be overcome, and moved out without conscious effort to the decision: 'I will go and find the Bushman.' The point may seem hardly worth labouring, but the principle, that the adult human spirit suffers no determination (even from God) without its own consent, is of vital importance for much of what remains to be said about prayer.[6]

How many of us have been 'going round in circles' for years in the matter of our relations with God. The decision by which we become, in Grou's meaning of the word, devout, is the 'break out' (to borrow once again from Colonel Van der Post) from this magic circle. Once made, it is so simple that we may well feel amazed that we had hesitated so long. What has held us back?

In very many cases, it has been not so much a particular attachment to some creaturely end which we recognised to be inconsistent with devotion. It has been an unparticularised fear; a fear of cutting our moorings, and of the unknown ocean beyond our familiar land-locked harbour. It is the fear of the heart-shaking 'tremendous mystery'; a horror of having to await, naked, the 'uplifted stroke' of divine love.[7] How clever of the Communists to describe religion as the opium of the people, when all the time in fact we use the things of this world to drug our apprehension, lest we should be compelled

---

[6]A great deal has been written about 'passive' prayer, and this by authors of the highest intrinsic and extrinsic authority; and a distinction is frequently propounded between 'active' or 'acquired' contemplation and passive contemplation. Such language may be useful for the purpose of contrasting different psychological states and for spiritual diagnosis. They are of no ultimate philosophical or theological significance. On the contrary: (a) the most 'passive' kind of prayer is not prayer at all unless it is underwritten by the consent of the 'patient', and by this consent transformed into his own vital act; (b) even the most active kind of prayer, the stumbling effort of the veriest beginner, or of the sinner who has not repented, is a supernatural gift of God, something 'received' from God and accepted from him by the co-operation of the person with an actual grace.

[7]*The Hound of Heaven.* I understand that Francis Thompson is still 'out' poetically. But he knew something about love and religion.

to face the reality of God. We have been like a child who
frightens himself with bogies in the candle-light, and then
rushes to hide his head beneath the bed-clothes. What is more
terrible than God, love, infinitely demanding, because infinitely pure — until we surrender to his invitation? Until that
invitation is heard, and unless it is answered, we are still
dealing with God as a factor in our situation. But in a sense
God is not a factor in any situation; he *is* the situation, and it
seems terrible to face the truth at last. 'Do not let us hear the
Lord speaking; it will cost us our lives' (Exodus xx. 19). And
yet:

> There is a tide in the affairs of men
> Which, taken at the flood, leads on to fortune.
> Omitted, all the voyage of their life
> Is bound in shallows and in miseries.

It is true, as Plato said, there is no place for envy in the
pageantry of heaven. Often enough, the divine invitation,
neglected once and again, is again repeated. But if we go on
rejecting it, the last invitation will pass us by. 'If it were done,
'twere well it were done quickly.'

And when it *is* done? It may be, of course, that the decision,
having once been taken, the man who is thus disposed 'to do
everything and to suffer everything for God' will quickly
realise that, for him, this involves a whole change of the
external conditioning of life. Good 'vocations' to the so-called
'religious' life of monks and nuns often spring from the
disposition of devotion. And short of such a step, it is quite
likely that the devout man will come to see that a good many
minor adjustments in his way of life are called for. But it is
above all important to realise — and here the comparison

with Colonel Van der Post's case breaks down — that essentially the surrender of which we have been thinking, and the disposition to which it gives birth, are not concerned with anything in particular at all; or rather they are concerned with everything. Devotion means handing God a blank cheque, not knowing how he will fill it in. It means the substitution of God's will for anything that I might have felt inclined to will myself. But God's will is essentially mysterious to us. A particular way of life may be conducive to the fulfilment of God's will — or it may not. But even if it is, it is conducive as a means and not as an end. The end is precisely the further deepening and growth of the new-found relationship of our wills with God. This relationship is a relationship of love, of self-identification with God. It is capable of indefinite growth; and the closer we grow to God, the wider the vista that will open up before us.

We have to learn to laugh at our fears. After all, if we cannot trust the very source and origin of all good, the Lord of history, what chance is there of finding happiness anywhere else?

> Lo, all things fly thee, for thou fliest Me!
> Strange, piteous, futile thing!

Yet the fear can be very potent, and that is perhaps why so often it is through the practice of 'prayerful pondering' and other prayerful communion with God that people gradually find built up in themselves the counterpoise of strength and aspiration that at last allows them to 'break out'. Once again, we see how intimately life and prayer are interconnected. And if prayer disposes us to the surrender to God, which is the birth of 'devotion', devotion in its turn is likely to lead to profound modifications in our life of prayer.

vi

Crisis

As was said in the fourth chapter, prayer is a highly personal activity, as personal as the art of a painter or the love of a young man for his beloved. It is therefore a form of activity about which we may formulate rules and some general principles, but one which nevertheless in actual life transcends any rules that we can devise.

Because complete personal integration is not something with which we begin our life, but rather the goal of our living, it is possible to distinguish in each of us an 'average' or 'routine' self, and the 'real' self. The world, with its laws and conventions, deals with us as though we were all much alike. In the rough and tumble of ordinary human business we become 'hands' or abstract 'employers', and as such we play our parts in life. We have our average self, with its recognisable habits, good or bad, its mannerisms, its largely automatic likes and dislikes, its attractive and unattractive features, its average reaction to the average claims of routine circumstance. The world wants us to be stable and dependable units in the structure of its society, and we respond to this demand. We make a husk, a hard outer shell, for ourselves, a shield and shelter against the harsh wind of circumstance. We adopt a 'pose', a mask; and when it does its work we grow more and more into it. It deceives the world about us, and may in the end deceive ourselves. Have we not, most of us, amongst our circle of acquaintance, someone who has adopted such a pose so successfully that he no longer seems able to dissociate himself from it even in his own thought? Some sudden crisis, peril or opportunity may, however, occasionally surprise the real self within us, and for a moment we appear in our true colours. Our friends and enemies are then ready enough to comment: 'I never thought he had it in him.'

It is characteristic of love that it can pierce our masks and see us for what we really are. Love is not blind. Profound love, on the contrary, is very perspicacious and sees both the weakness and the real hidden strength of the beloved.

Prayer, as in these pages we have been coming to understand it, is the response of our love to God's love for us. The living God, then, is the 'other side' of prayer. And God, the living and the loving One, is interested in our real self rather than in our outward semblance. He is, as the Bible puts it, 'the searcher of hearts'. His love for us logically antecedes and creates our love for him, and its tendency is always to perfect in us that complete interior surrender which is the condition of full union between our will and his.

Each of us, then, beneath the conventional surface of our lives, is a unique person. Prayer is a willed or consented relation between this unique person and God. It follows that prayer is something different for each of us, something that, in the last resort, each of us has to learn neither from books nor from oral advice but from God himself. Books and advice are useful, as we shall emphasise later on, but they cannot take the place of the interior guidance of the Holy Spirit.

This means that even the most general rules that can be offered are to be taken with a certain liberty of spirit and to be adapted to the personal vocation of the person who is trying to pray. We have to be prepared to be experimental in prayer, to find out, by trial and error, what suits our needs, to pray in the way which we find possible for ourselves and not to mind if we find that we cannot pray as others whom we admire seem to pray. Provided that we are genuinely seeking God and his will, we can be sure that God will bless our efforts and our experiments and will lead us into the paths that he has destined for us. And in fact, from the moment that we are genuinely trying to pray and to learn how to pray better, his grace is working in us and the union with him for which we long has already been begun . 'Thou wouldst not be seeking me if thou hadst not already found me.'

One word of advice can hardly be misplaced. It is that we should not get preoccupied with the question of the extent of our progress in the way of prayer. There is a vast number of valuable (and some pernicious) books on prayer and the spiritual life. In fact there is a 'science' of the spiritual life, and authors vie with one another in distinguishing stages in it. But this should not lead us to start worrying about what stage we ourselves have reached — the 'purgative' way, the 'illumina-tive' way, or the 'unitive' way, and so forth. We are not good judges of our own spiritual condition. It is not required of us that we should know these things. And to want to know shows an introspective curiosity and concern about ourselves which is at the opposite role from true prayer. Prayer is not concerned to discover how good we are. Its concern is the goodness of God; it is directed outwards and upwards, not inwards to ourselves, and as its object is infinite it is always more conscious of the journey that lies before it than of the road already traversed. If we find that, while the adventure of prayer goes on, we are growing more deeply, though still peacefully, aware of the disparity between our ideals and our life, and of the claims of our neighbour upon our active love, then it is probable that there is little basically wrong with our prayer.

With these thoughts in our mind, we can revert to the subject of 'prayerful pondering' which occupied us in Chapter IV. The person who has been brought to the decision and disposition of 'devotion' described above will not improbably find that, as a result, his pondering on the things of God and the prayer that springs from it have become much more meaningful, and have been, in a sense, facilitated. He is loving God in a new and deeper way and he may feel a greater attraction to dwell in mind on God and the mysteries of religion and to address himself to God in adoration, love and trust. The quiet pauses in his time of prayer will also, probably, seem more worth while, and they may come to occupy more of the total period, with excellent results.

It might be supposed that from this point onwards the development of prayer would be straightforward and would keep to the lines on which, with the practice of 'prayerful pondering', it had so fruitfully started. For some people, and for most, if not all of their subsequent life, this may be true. The imagination may become more vivid, the understanding more far-ranging and penetrative, the response of the emotions warmer and more reliable, the direct prayer to God in recognisable acts of adoration, thanksgiving, love, penitence and petition easier and more intimate. Such persons need perhaps mainly to be warned against excessive emotionalism, and a use of the imagination which is rather artistic or poetic than religious, a use of the understanding which is theological rather than devout.

Experience; however, shows that in very many cases the development of the life of prayer is not of this straightforward, non-problematic, kind. Although prayer is an activity corresponding to the deepest bent of a nature made by God for union with himself, and despite the fact that by grace we receive a supernatural endowment for the pursuit of this union, many people are far from finding prayer a delightful and easy practice. On the contrary, they find it extremely difficult and wearisome. And especially, complaints are frequent that 'meditation' and 'mental prayer' are too hard to be persevered with.

There are even those to whom the practice of 'meditation' or 'prayerful pondering' seems abnormally difficult, almost impossible, even from the start. Anyone can, of course, on occasion, imagine a Gospel scene and think about its meaning or message — just as one can imagine a scene from Dickens. But quite a number of people find it most unrewarding to try to do this at set times and for set periods daily, and to make this a natural introduction to actual praying.

Others will say that they were at one time able to use this method of prayer, that they got great satisfaction out of it, and that they found it a real help and inspiration for their spiritual life. But that time is now past. Their present predicament is that when the attempt is made to practise mental prayer, their mind and imagination, their emotions, and even their will, seem to go entirely blank, arid and lifeless. They may even go so far as to tell themselves 'I cannot pray. Prayer is something for very good people, or for professional people like monks and nuns. I am a very ordinary sort of person, a private soldier in the army of God, and I must leave the higher flights for my superiors.' They would perhaps be surprised to learn that 'inability to pray' afflicts the professionals too, and can cause them great anguish and distress. In any case, one cannot accept a division of people into 'first-class' and 'second-class' children of God.

The reason for such inability to pray may, in any given case, be a deliberate failure of the will. Prayer is the expression of a relationship with God, the essence of which, on the human side, is unqualified adoration and love. A typical act of prayer might be formulated in the words: 'My God, I love you above all things and for your own sake.' It is obviously going to be very difficult to pray such a prayer with meaning and any sense of satisfaction, if in fact one does not so love God and is not even trying to do so. Such a love of God necessarily involves an element of self-sacrifice, and anyone who is consciously refusing a type or degree of self-sacrifice which he knows God is here and now asking of him can expect to find prayer an unrewarding, unsatisfactory, arid, and rather futile activity. Shakespeare has illustrated the point very vividly in the soliloquy of the remorseful but (so far) unrepentant king in *Hamlet*:

> *Oh my offence is rank, it smells to heaven,*
> It hath the primal eldest curse upon it,

A brother's murder, *Pray can I not,*
Though inclination be as sharp as will:
My stronger guilt defeats my strong intent.
. . . . . But oh, what form of prayer
Can serve my turn? 'Forgive me my foul murder'?
That cannot be, since I am still possess'd
Of those effects for which I did the murder.

It should be noticed that the failure of will in question here is a refusal of a sacrifice which God is *here and now* asking of us. God's requirements are adjusted to the stage of development of the individual person. A beginner is not usually required to give up immediately all that a saint may be asked to renounce. But if either the beginner or the saint is deliberately refusing to surrender to God something that he knows God wishes him to give up here and now, then he is likely to run into difficulties in prayer which cannot be surmounted so long as he is 'still possess'd' of what for him is no longer compatible with a genuine and efficacious love of God above all things.

To suppose, on the other hand, that the kind of 'inability to pray' of which we are speaking is always due to such a failure of good will would be both cruel and untrue. There is overwhelming evidence to the contrary, and indeed it is often the 'devout' person who comes up against this difficulty, with nothing to explain it either in his spiritual imperfections or his physical condition. Not infrequently, it is a symptom of a crisis in spiritual growth. As we have seen, there is a connection between our prayer-life and the rest of our life. This connection becomes more intimate when the surrender of which we spoke in Chapter V has brought the will under closer habitual subordination to the will of God. 'Devotion' is a disposition capable of indefinite growth, and, as in the physical order, spiritual growth has both its continuity and its discontinuities, both of which are likely to find their reflection in the prayer-life of the individual concerned.

Leaving aside, then, the person whose trouble is a deliberate failure to adjust his will to the requirements of the love of God, we have to consider the needs alike of the 'devout' person who, after successful practice of 'pondering' or 'meditative' prayer, finds that this is no longer possible or fruitful for him, and of the 'beginner' who cannot even start a successful habit of such meditation.

It is probable enough that the psychological diagnosis of the inability in these two different types may itself be different. But the practical recommendations are much the same, and to these we will now turn.

Let us begin by asking a question: Do you *want* to pray? The question seems a silly one, but it is crucial. 'Of course', you say, 'I want to pray. Why else do you suppose that I searched around for a "method" that would suit me, and tried to use such a method?' And then you will add, either 'But I have never been able to find one', or 'I did find such a method, and for a time it seemed to work. But now, it has left me in the lurch. I want to pray even more than I did when I first began to do so. I want God. In fact, there is nothing else that I do want absolutely, however many things I find relatively attractive. But my imagination seems to have become barren. My thoughts won't express themselves. I have lost all feeling for God or religious practices. My very will seems dead, and I feel helpless before the assaults of temptations which I thought I had conquered forever. I hope I still believe in God and his revelation. But it all seems quite empty and meaningless to me;

I don't even know what I *mean* by "God". What can I do? No method seems to help me now, and I am tempted to give up the effort to pray. Probably I was never meant for these high things. Presumably I'm just a mediocre sort of person, who will be lucky if he just manages to qualify for salvation in the end.'

So far from being silly, our question ('Do you want to pray?') has brought us to the very heart of the whole matter. *To want to pray is the heart of prayer.* Without it, no prayer is of much value. But provided we want to pray, we retain the essence of prayer even though all the expected concomitants of that desire appear to have deserted us. The value of prayer is the reality of the intention to pray.

Let us suppose, for the sake of argument, that you have had not only a method but a rule of prayer. Obeying this rule, you set aside half an hour in the day for prayer. You go before the Blessed Sacrament, or to your bedside, or out into the garden, or whatever your practice is. You make the sign of the Cross. You make an act of faith in God's presence.[1] You say to him (in effect, or *in intention*): This half-hour is all for you; help me, while it lasts, to forget the distracting delights and problems of my world; help me to forget my spiritual troubles; help me to remember you and your love; help me to tell you that I love you, or at least want to love you; pour your love into me, and help me to love you more.

In other words, what have you done, what are you doing? You are making it your real intention to attend to God for half

---

[1]This does not mean that one 'feels' God's presence, whether in oneself or in the Blessed Sacrament. It simply means a recognition that he *is* present, feeling or no feeling. In the 'crisis' it is quite likely that one will 'feel' that he is entirely absent, even non-existent.

an hour. You find that you cannot imagine holy things; you cannot think about God or holy things. You try to attend to God as he is in himself, the God of your faith. But you seem to be in great darkness. You have no sense of God's presence, no idea of what he is like. Your intention to attend to God seems to result, in practice, in attending to a sheer void. And soon you discover the fact that your imagination or your mind has been caught and carried away by some silly distraction — some mental picture or some thought of a subject that affects you in your exterior life, or even something that is of no significance at all. You try again to attend to the unseen, unfelt God, and again you 'wake up' to find that you have been distracted. Perhaps at the end of the half-hour you have to admit that twenty-eight of its minutes have been spent in involuntary distractions.

What you have to realise is that these distractions — involuntary, as we have supposed them to be — do not matter. They do not interrupt your real prayer. Your real prayer is your intention to pray, your intention to give this half-hour over to attending to God. You intended to attend to him. You probably renewed that intention from time to time, when you became aware that you had been distracted, and tried to turn your attention back to God. *At no time did you retract your intention.* In that case, your intention has been continuous. It has been there, hidden, as it were, beneath a heap of involuntary distractions. You have, then, been praying for half an hour. A very odd sort of prayer, you may say. It may have given you very little satisfaction. You may feel ashamed of having 'put up such a poor show'. But this prayer, with which you are so dissatisfied, has given God a great deal of satisfaction. What God is interested in is not so much what goes on or does not go on in your imagination or your reason, but rather your intention to pray, your *will* to give him half an hour of your time.

We have to apply to the question of prayer the tests which we should agree to be valid in other matters. Suppose a man decides to commit a murder at a place five miles away, and sets out to walk to the scene of the intended crime. Every step he takes to that goal is sinful, because the motive of it is to enable him to commit the murder. If he is the sort of person who 'takes murder in his stride', it may well be that during large parts of the journey the surface of his mind is occupied with quite other thoughts. But these thoughts do not excuse him. Stop him at any point of his journey and ask him what he is doing, and (in the unlikely event that he tells you the truth) he will reply that he is on his way to commit a murder. The *moral significance* of his journey, at every stage of it, is determined by the intention which governs it.

So it is with our set periods of prayer. Their moral (and religious) significance is determined by the intention which governs them; and if that intention has been a formed and unretracted intention to pray, then any such period has been a period of uninterrupted prayer.

The question of distractions may deserve a little further consideration. We all experience distractions in mental work. One sets out to compose an after-dinner speech, and after a time one finds that one's mind has 'wandered' to yesterday's bicycle ride or tomorrow's board meeting. And so it is, unfortunately often, with prayer. Broadly speaking, there are three sorts of distraction in prayer:

(1) There is the fully voluntary distraction. I begin to pray, but (finding it a dull and boring occupation) I decide to think,

instead, of how I shall amuse myself in my next period of recreation. Notice: I *decide* to think of some worldly interest. It is a deliberate voluntary decision. The thoughts that result from it are *intentionally* irrelevant to prayer. Such distractions of course interrupt prayer. But they are not a problem. *We need not have voluntary distractions;* and if we want to pray we shall not admit them.

(2) At the other extreme, there are what one may describe as floating wisps of involuntary distractions. They are analogous to the irrelevant noises — a fly buzzing, or a distant door slamming, while one is listening enraptured to some piece of magnificent and absorbing music. So, too, in prayer, the image of a human friend may pass across the surface of our consciousness, or a vague wonder what the weather is going to be this evening. The only course to follow in regard to these wisps of distraction is to do nothing at all about them. They are not destroying our attention to God, and provided we do nothing about them they will fade away. If, on the other hand, we turn deliberately to the task of suppressing them, we are diverting our attention from God to attend to the distractions. Similarly, when we are listening to music, if we turn our deliberate thought and attention from the music to the buzzing fly, then the fly has won the day.

(3) Distinct from both these kinds of distraction are the big, absorbing, but *involuntary* distractions which seem to take possession of us unawares and to have occupied the whole forefront of our consciousness. It is quite true, of course, that if we were holier people than we are, if we had more thoroughly detached ourselves from all created ends, so that nothing but God could really attract our will, we might be less subject to such distractions. On the other hand, distractions often arise

from the necessary commitments of our daily life, from business which is truly God's business because it is part of our service of God and others. The housewife, the engineer, the school-teacher, may be anything but inordinately attached to the matters of daily work; but these matters may yet come to plague any one of them in his or her prayer. Whatever the source and ultimate cause of these involuntary but absorbing distractions, the point is that *here and now* we are not responsible for them. They are against our will. Our actual will is to attend to God. Outside prayer, it will be well if we try to remove from our lives the sources of distraction that are unnecessary, and for which therefore we carry some responsibility. But during prayer, what matters is our deliberate intention to attend to God, our intention to pray. Distracted prayer, when the distractions are involuntary, can be very painful to nature, very mortifying, and so very purifying. But the important thing to remember is that, despite the distractions, it is really prayer.

The heart of prayer, then, is this intention to pray. And the act of prayer is essentially the act of giving oneself to God, the act of surrender. In the quaint words of *The Epistle of Counsel*:

> Think simply that thou art as thou art, be thou never so foul nor so wretched, so that thou have beforetimes (as I suppose that thou hast) been lawfully amended of all thy sins in special and in general, after the true counsel of Holy Church.[2] ... And although thou feel thyself yet then so vile and wretched, that for cumberance of thyself thou knowest not thyself what is

---

[2] i.e., provided that you have been absolved from all your grave sins in the sacrament of penance.

best for thee to do with thyself, this then shalt thou do as I bid thee.

Take good gracious God as he is, plat and plain as a plaster, and lay it on to thy sick self as thou art. Or, if I shall say otherwise, bear up thy sick self as thou art and try for to touch by desire good, gracious God as He is . . . without any curious or special beholding to any of the qualities that belong to the being of thyself or of God, whether they be clean or wretched, gracious or natural, godly or manly. It mattereth not now to thee, but that thy blind beholding of thy naked being be gladly borne up in lustiness of love to be knitted and oned in grace and in spirit to the precious Being of God in himself as he is, without more.[3]

The beginner who has never been able to practise the 'prayerful pondering' of which we spoke in Chapter IV, and the person who, having once been able to 'meditate', can do so no longer, will probably feel the need of some more detailed suggestions.

The period of set prayer should be approached in a spirit of humble reliance, not on one's own capacity to pray, but on the mercy of God who calls us to prayer, gives us the will to pray, and responds to that will by further outpourings of his grace. The prayer may then begin by the formation of an actual intention to devote the period to attending to God. The reader has already been warned that there is an element of paradox in 'attending' to a Reality which transcends all our powers of picturing and conceiving. It is likely that one will seem to be

---

[3]*The Cloud of Unknowing and Other Treatises*, Orchard Series, pp. 185f. (1924 edition).

attending to a Void or a Nothing. But, as *The Cloud of Unknowing* says:

> Although thy bodily wits can find there nothing to feed them on, for they think it nought that thou dost, yea! do on then this nought, and do it for God's love. And cease not, therefore, but travail busily in that nought with a watchful desire to have God, whom no man can know.[4]

Many of those who practise this kind of prayer find that it is helpful to intersperse it with very brief and simple 'acts' (which need not be spoken acts) of adoration, love, penitence, trust, desire, resignation. These acts may be of one's own invention, or they may be drawn from the Psalms or other sources, e.g.:

Lord, have mercy.
God, be merciful to me, a sinner.
Heal me, Lord, and I shall be healed.
Lord, I am not worthy, but speak the word only,
    and I shall be healed.
I adore thee, Hidden God.
Glory be to the Holy Trinity.
Lord, I am nothing; thou art All.
In thee have I trusted, let me never be confounded.
Though he slay me, yet will I trust in him.
I want thee and thy will; there is nothing that I want
    in comparison with thee.
Thy will be done.
Be it done unto me, according to thy word.

[4] P. 159 (1924 edition).

Not my will, but thine.
My spirit rejoices in God my saviour.
I rejoice that thou are infinitely happy,
Jesus.

The above are of course only samples. One should make one's own choice of such 'acts'. They should be so familiar to us that we can use them without thinking closely about our selection of them or about their contents. If we can get on with a very few such acts, so much the better. The same act can be repeated from time to time, and we should pause between each act or each repetition:

Let the acts come. Do not force them. They ought *not* to be *fervent*, excited, anxious, but calm, simple, unmeaning, unfelt. .
The acts will tend to be *always the same.* The first stage is usually (I think): — 'I am a miserable sinner: have mercy on me', or something to this effect. But the *principal* stage consists of this: 'O God, I want Thee, and I do not want anything else.'[5]
It is important to remember that such acts, though they are a help to prayer (for some people), are not the essence of the kind of prayer we are here talking about, but only an aid and a concomitant. The essence of the prayer is the intention to attend to God. The meaning of the words of the acts is not, therefore, to be dwelt on with assiduity or curiosity. We are not to make toilsome efforts to conjure up feelings or emotions appropriate to the wording of the acts. If we find that the acts seem to lose any particular meaning, that is excellent. We may also come to realise that it is one thing to say 'I love thee with

---

[5]*Contemplative Prayer; a Few Simple Rules,* by H. J. Chapman, printed as an appendix to his *Spiritual letters* (p. 289).

all my heart', and another thing actually so to love God. We may then realise that all that we can really do for ourselves (with the help of grace) in our prayer is to *dispose* ourselves for God's action upon and within us: 'Patiently I waited for the Lord's help, and at last he turned his look towards me; he listened to my plea' (Psalms xxxix. 2). If we can learn to wait in silence and darkness upon God, our will attached to nothing else but Him, we are in a good way of prayer.

vii

Books

If you wish to become a physicist, an engineer, or an architect, you will be well advised to study what has already been achieved in the field of your choice. The sciences, the crafts, and the arts have each their tradition of acquired knowledge and inherited skills. If you choose to disregard the tradition and to become an engineer 'starting from scratch', you will be lucky if you get as far as Archimedes the ancient Greek, who discovered the lever. Meanwhile, your fellow-engineers, who have been willing to learn from tradition, will have accepted from it both the lever and a host of other inventions and principles, and you yourself will never be able to catch up with them.

It is true that progress depends on going beyond what tradition has taught. But the normal method of progress is to accept from tradition and, on that basis, to proceed further. The innovator may appear to his contemporaries to be a revolutionary, a rejector of tradition. But the best revolutions have usually accepted far more from the past than even their contrivers realised. And when the revolutionary spirit is exaggerated, so that it becomes a rejection of tradition for no other reason than that it is traditional, the results are usually deplorable.

There is a great tradition of the spiritual life and the life of prayer — in fact, there are several such, if we include in our view not only the Christian religion but the great faiths of the East and the Near East. This tradition is partly embodied in a vast literature, and partly carried on, as all human traditions are, in and by a common way of life, oral teaching, and the direct transmission of what, in this sphere, corresponds to the methods and skills of the traditional sciences and arts.

For a Christian, of course, this tradition is essential to his Christian faith. The Christian faith centres in the historical fact of the life and death and resurrection of Jesus of Nazareth, a fact which is brought to our knowledge not by immediate revelation to each of us, but intermediately through tradition, as all historical facts are. This tradition, we believe, was entrusted from the start to the society instituted by Christ, the Church or Messianic Community. In the Church it is preserved; and in and by the Church and her members its implications are investigated. The 'mustard seed' of the gospel thus grows up and becomes the 'tree' of the total traditional knowledge and wisdom of the Church.

The Church's tradition is crystallised for us primarily in the books of the New Testament, which are not only the earliest extant written records of it, but have the unique status of being divinely inspired. These books, and especially the Gospels, afford us a treasury of material for 'prayerful pondering'.

The New Testament was followed by a mass of early Christian literature, of which considerable fragments survive, among them one or two early treatises on prayer.

The fourth Christian century, in which the Church emerged from the constant threat of persecution as an 'illicit religion', to become, before A.D. 400, the established religion of the Roman Empire, witnessed the astonishing phenomenon of the 'flight to the desert'. In growing numbers, fervent Christians escaped from the corrupt society of a decadent Empire and from the lowered standards of average Christian life (for Christianity had ceased to be a heroic option, and conformity to the new imperial religion could be a means to worldly advancement), and sought a closer union with God in the austere solitudes of the Egyptian and Syrian deserts. 'Monasticism' was born, and a great impetus was given to the production and dissemination of books on the spiritual life and on the practice of prayer. What has survived of the literature of the 'Fathers of the desert' is a curious farrago, ranging from the heights of a spiritual insight which has rarely been surpassed to depths of absurdity and eccentricity. Some of the best elements in this spirituality of the desert have been preserved for us in the writings of John Cassian (early fifth century), which so greatly influenced St Benedict and, through him and by reason of his encouragement, the whole of the great medieval monastic tradition.

The later Middle Ages in the West were also deeply, and increasingly, influenced by the writings of the self-styled 'Dionysius the Areopagite', actually a writer of about A.D. 500. His sublime teaching was utilised not only by such writers as the great unknown English author of *The Cloud of Unknowing* and *The Epistle of Privy Counsels* (fourteenth-century masterpieces of instruction on prayer), but had a great part to play in the theological synthesis of St Thomas Aquinas (*c.* A.D. 1250).

The period immediately preceding the Reformation was one of spiritual decline, of pessimism and of individualism — tendencies which have left their mark even on the famous *Imitation of Christ.* It was, however, followed, in the generations which actually witnessed the establishment of the Reformation bodies, by a wonderful revival of which the two great standard-bearers were St Teresa of Avila and her disciple St John of the Cross. A little earlier, St Ignatius of Loyola had founded the Society of Jesus, which became the great exponent and disseminator of the technique of formal meditation.

The three saints just mentioned all came from the Iberian peninsula. But the next great epoch of spiritual literature was predominantly French, though fecundated by the Spanish revival. St Francis de Sales and Benet Fitch of Canfield (an Englishman who lived and worked in France) may be said to head the list of a series of writers which only ended with the Jesuit Père Grou at the end of the eighteenth century.

The nineteenth century was again a period of decline. But towards its end Leo XIII initiated the revival of Thomist philosophy and theology, and this (together with his successor's emphasis on frequent communion and the phenomenal influence of the autobiography of the Carmelite Saint Thérèse of Lisieux) probably had much to do with the great recovery of interest in the theory and practice of prayer in the twentieth century.

The field of choice for spiritual reading is thus a very extensive one, so extensive indeed as to be embarrassing for the newcomer. The following suggestions for reading may be helpful to some, but the principles governing them should be understood.

These suggestions, to begin with, inevitably reflect the limited reading experiences and tastes of the present writer. And they have been determined by the presumed needs of Anglo-Saxon readers who want their books to be in English. The list is not meant to be in any sense exclusive; nor should the omission of any particular book or writer be taken as implying disapproval.

The requirements of those who use the method of 'prayerful pondering' are somewhat different from those of others who use the less imaginative, less intellectual, way of prayer outlined in the previous chapter. For the former, the New Testament, and especially the Gospels, are of course the great treasure-house of seminal images. Those who find that they are more drawn to reasoning than to imagining may get much help from the *Imitation of Christ*, a work which needs no recommendation, but does require a certain amount of discretion on the part of the reader.[1] And both the thinkers and the imaginers will profit by reading St Francis de Sales' *Introduction to the Devout Life*. This little book was of immense historical importance. One of the chronic dangers to which Christianity is, it seems, exposed is that serious prayer and the serious practice of the spiritual life come to be looked upon as a monopoly of the 'professionally religious'. A large proportion

---

[1] As an example, we may take the celebrated observation of the author of the *Imitation*: 'I had rather have compunction than know the definition thereof.' This preference is, in itself, unexceptionable. But one may reflect that it would be best of all to have compunction *and* to know its definition. The dangers of an immortified esteem and pursuit of learning and speculation are obvious, but we are not therefore to take refuge in obscurantism.

of Christian spiritual literature has been written for nuns or monks by monks or nuns. It has used the jargon of the cloisters and presupposed the conditions of the cloistered life. Yet Christ himself had directed his mission not specially to the professionally religious but to those whom the professionally religious looked down upon as 'the people of the land' or even as 'sinners'. St Francis de Sales was not a monk but a diocesan bishop, equally at home in the cottage of a Savoy peasant and at the courts of princes. The *Introduction* deliberately aims at Christians living 'in the world', not to take them out of the world into the cloister (as St Bernard would have hoped to do), but to encourage and help them to seek the heights of union with God in their worldly surroundings. The book rapidly became a best-seller and has continued ever since to give inspiration to the kind of readers for whom it was originally intended.

What of the needs of those who pray without much recourse to the imagination or the reasoning faculty? They are threefold.

(1) The imagination and the reason must not be starved. But they are not being fed in the set periods of prayer, in which the contribution of the creature tends to be little more than an activity of the will guided by the obscure light of 'blind' faith. Hence, it is good, from time to time, to take, for spiritual reading outside the set times of prayer, the same sort of books that are immediately useful for the prayer of those who 'ponder'. The same purpose may be served by occasionally reading the life of a saint or other great Christian. There is a wealth of such biographies for every taste, from major works like Fr Brodrick's great life of St Ignatius of Loyola to Goodier's *Saints for Sinners* and the series of bedtime saints. Those who

have the literary and spiritual perception to penetrate a rather repugnant surface of sentimentality and childishness will find, in the autobiography of St Thérèse of Lisieux, a message of profound and heroic holiness, holiness made accessible to everyone by the saint's teaching on utter trust in God and on finding expressions of our love for him, not primarily in what the world would judge to be great actions or great sufferings, but in the opportunities afforded by the trivialities of a humdrum routine. But if the *Autobiography* is not to the reader's taste, he can study the saint in Görres' *The Hidden Face.*

(2) One of the great needs of those who try to lead a life of prayer is of something to fortify their courage, to animate their efforts, and to encourage them to persevere. Well-chosen lives of saints may again be helpful in this connection. But there is much else besides:

Grou's *A Manual for Interior Souls* is, despite its forbidding title, a book of the very greatest value. It is in the best tradition of French spirituality. It is pungent, bracing and wise. The reader should however observe that its tone is somewhat rhetorical, reflecting perhaps the art of the preacher.

St Francis de Sales' *Conferences* were addressed to nuns. Provided that allowance is made for this fact, they are an admirable introduction to the spirit of this great saint.

The works of Father Robert Steuart, and along with them *Father Steuart*, by Katherine Kendall, are useful both in general and also as giving sound instruction on prayer in a thoroughly Anglo-Saxon way.

St John of the Cross is a master of the spiritual life and of prayer. But he is very easily misunderstood, and his poetic, Spanish, counter-reformation temperament makes him a difficult author for many modern readers. Rather than recommend any of his own books, I would suggest *St John of the Cross*, by Father Gabriel. The author of this study is a member of St John of the Cross's own Reformed Carmelite Order, and a most perceptive, sympathetic and prudent critic. The translation is not without blemishes.

Bremond's *History of Religious Thought in France* is, unfortunately, not translated into English, except for the first few volumes. It was a major achievement, written over a period of many years, during which the author's own insight into the themes of prayer and the spiritual life developed enormously. Some of the later volumes contain work which has rarely been surpassed.

De Caussade was a Jesuit of the mid-eighteenth century. His *Abandonment to Divine Providence* and *Spiritual Letters* are pure gold. The former has an adventitious quality, not found in all good spiritual books: it is a superb piece of literature. There are people who, having once 'discovered' de Caussade, return to him over and over again with unfailing relish and a sense that here they have been brought face to face with the essence of religion and the gospel.

(3) If poetry is something more than the art of versification, it is still more true that prayer is not a technique. Yet something can be learnt from books that deal with the question: how to pray, one or two of which may be mentioned here. *The Two Voices*, a posthumous collection of spiritual addresses by Robert Steuart, devotes its third part to the subject of prayer.

De Caussade, *On Prayer* (Burns and Oates, 2nd edition; the first edition included many mistranslations). The first part of this book is a brilliant and subtle theological discussion of the differences between the teaching of orthodox masters of the subject of prayer and the errors of the Quietists. The ordinary modern reader (if also a Christian) is not very likely to fall by accident into quietism; the temptation is rather to be too activist. The reader may therefore disregard the first part and go straight to Part II, which gives instructions on prayer by one of the very greatest of the orthodox masters. Piquancy is added to the book by its author's constant appeal to the authority of Bossuet.

Difficulties of Mental Prayer, by Father Boylan, may be most warmly recommended.

References have already been made to *The Cloud of Unknowing* and *The Epistle of Privy Counsel*, by an anonymous Englishman of the fourteenth century. This unknown author was a very great master of the subject of prayer. His beautiful English has been discreetly modernised in Justin McCann's *Orchard Series* edition of the two treatises; this volume includes a valuable commentary on *The Cloud* by the seventeenth-century English Benedictine, Augustine Baker, whose own spiritual teaching (deeply influenced by that of *The Cloud*) is preserved in the compilation *Holy Wisdom*. *The Cloud* is not an easy book to understand, and should be read meditatively and frequently re-read, not forgetting the advice of the author that one should 'take time to read it . . . all over. For peradventure there is some matter therein, in the beginning or in the middle, the which is hanging and not fully declared where it standeth; and if it be not there, it is soon after, or else in the end. Wherefore, if a man saw one matter and not another, peradventure he might lightly be led into error.' *The Epistle of Privy Counsel* is in some ways easier to understand, and hardly less valuable, than the more famous major work.

The selection of titles given above may serve as an introduction to the enormous wealth of literature on the subject of prayer and the spiritual life, which is one of the greatest heirlooms of the Church. Other books will suggest themselves to the student. One will be well advised to confine himself to authors approved as orthodox by the Church. There are honest blunderers, as well as charlatans, in the field of spiritual teaching, as in the fields of art, science and history; and their errors sometimes require the eye of a trained theologian to detect them.

A few general remarks on 'spiritual reading' may be useful. Anyone who is trying to make prayer a real and substantial part of his life should make a regular practice of such reading, even if it is only a quarter of an hour a day. The reading should not be done as a substitute for prayer, but in addition to it.

Everyone has his own tastes, depending on personal association, natural temperament, and his own progress. Some, for instance, are repelled by the extremely prosaic approach of Augustine Baker. Others will be put off by the markedly poetic vein of *The Cloud*. Those who enjoy the feminine humour and buoyancy of St Teresa (of Avila) are balanced by those who find the theological masculinity of St John of the Cross more to their liking. St John of the Cross was in fact a great poet; but in his own explanations of his poems he manages to be very unpoetic. Those who find the 'sweetness' of St Francis de Sales cloying may prefer the salt flavour of *The Manual for Interior Souls*. It is a good principle to be guided to a great extent by one's own taste, while occasionally deviating into other regions, for change and contrast. It is a great help if, in course of time, one can come to concentrate (not exclusively but specially) on a few authors, or even one; but they, or he, should be chosen with mature judgment, and in full recognition of the fact that, later on, pride of place may come to be given to a different selection of literature.

One warning is universally applicable. The advices and examples which are contained in spiritual books are only to be followed and imitated to the extent that the judgment and conscience of the reader find them genuinely appropriate to his own case. There is, in the lives of the saints, as has been well said, a great deal that is admirable without therefore being imitable: 'When one is conscious of no attraction, no grace, for those marvellous things that make the saints admirable, one must be fair to oneself and say: "God asked these things from his saints; he does not ask them of me" ' (de Caussade). What is true of the lives of the saints is true of spiritual literature in general. Each of us is unique. God does not ask us to go to him by a general but by a particular path. That path will be made clear to us not from books, though perhaps with the help of books. Provided that we never stray from the infallible teaching of the Church in her official proclamation and exposition of the gospel, we shall do well to be more lavish of our admiration than our imitation. We can often be helped indirectly by teaching and examples which, however, are not directly appropriate to our own needs. It is good that a statesman should admire a general; but if he tries to play the part of a general in his political career, he is courting disaster.

An incidental profit to be gained from regular spiritual reading is the lesson it conveys that the Church is something more than a great visible institution, with its officials, its law, its system of administration, and its political implications. The inspiring principle of the Church is the Holy Spirit, and the effect of the mission of the Holy Spirit to mankind is the life in grace of the Church's members and of those whose goodwill would lead them to membership if they had the corresponding mental enlightenment. The life in grace is not primarily the life of ecclesiastical politics but the life of faith and hope and charity, the life of interior surrender to the sovereignty and love of God.

viii

Gurus & Guides

Literature is not the only vehicle of tradition. There is also oral teaching. Oral teaching and literature are complementary. A judicious selection of books can put each of us into contact with the profoundest minds, and with people of outstanding spiritual experience, not only of our own but of previous generations. But books are written, not as a rule for a single reader, and anyhow not for you or me in particular. And because we cannot interrogate their authors we can easily become the victims of our own misunderstanding of what has been written.[1] An individual teacher or guide will very likely be less wise and less experienced than the best authors within our range; but he has the enormous advantage of being able to assess our own problems and needs and to correct our misunderstanding of his teaching.

[1] Many authors would agree that even competent critics and reviewers have a remarkable liability to misinterpret what they read and to be blind to the main gist of a book.

The importance of a living spiritual guide (*guru*) has been very emphatically appreciated by the spiritual tradition of India. In that tradition 'the means of attaining to Being' — or as we should say, transposing into Western and Christian terminology, the *way to God* — are denominated *yoga*. And *yoga* requires the guidance of a *guru*:

> Strictly speaking, all the other 'systems of philosophy' — as, in fact, all traditional disciplines or crafts — are, in India, taught by masters and are thus initiations; for millenniums they have been transmitted orally, 'from mouth to ear'. But Yoga is even more markedly initiatory in character. For, as in other religious initiations, the yogin begins by forsaking the profane world (family, society) and, guided by his *guru*, applies himself to passing successively beyond the behaviour patterns and values proper to the human condition.[2]
>
> The rule that respect be shown to a spiritual teacher is very old in India. In ancient times, perfect obedience was required from his pupil. He was the pupil's second father, more to be venerated than even his natural progenitor. Once, however, the state of pupillage was over, the obligation of obedience ceased, and only respect and gratitude were subsequently required. But in modern Hinduism this proper attitude is greatly exaggerated. While some of the sects . . . inculcate the greatest care in the selection of a guru, once selected he is to be obeyed implicitly throughout life.[3]

The rôle of the spiritual guide was similarly developed by the so-called Fathers of the Desert, to whom all subsequent

[2]Mircea Eliade, *Yoga, Immortality and Freedom*, Routledge and Kegan Paul, 1958, p. 5.
[3]G. A. Grierson, in *Encyclopaedia of Religion and Ethics*, Vol. 2, p. 546.

Christian spiritual teaching is so deeply indebted. As the Indian *guru* was his pupil's 'second father', so too the senior monk or hermit who instructed newcomers in the ways of prayer and asceticism was their spiritual 'father'. There are echoes of this Desert language in the Rule of St Benedict; not only are the young monks to revere their seniors as though they were their fathers, but in the opening words of the Prologue St. Benedict, who usually addresses his injunctions to the collective community, speaks in the singular number: 'Hear, my son, the precepts of your master, and incline the ear of your mind and gladly receive and effectually put into practice the advice of your tender father.' In more recent times great stress has been laid by spiritual writers on the importance of having a spiritual guide or 'director', and indeed the part assigned to this individual has not infrequently been exaggerated beyond the limits of what is desirable.

The great Jesuit Father Grou writes:

> To direct a soul is to lead it in the ways of God, it is to teach the soul to listen for the Divine inspiration and to respond to it; it is to suggest to the soul the practice of all the virtues proper for its particular state; it is not only to preserve that soul in purity and innocence, but to make it advance in perfection: in a word, it is to contribute as much as possibly may be in raising that soul to the degree of sanctity which God has destined for it. It is thus that Pope Saint Gregory thought of direction when he said that the guidance of souls is, of all the arts, the most excellent.
>
> Nothing is more important for souls who sincerely wish to give themselves entirely to God than, 1st, to be thoroughly convinced of the necessity of a director; 2nd, to make a good

choice of one; and, 3rd, to make use of him according to the designs of God, when they have once chosen him.[4]

There are phases in our life of prayer when a spiritual guide is specially desirable. When we first resolve to make a serious practice of prayer, we are probably so ignorant of what the life of prayer is that even the wisest of books may mislead us. Moreover, we are likely, at this initial stage, to discover difficulties and uncertainties to which we cannot find answers in the books. The help of a more experienced person is of enormous value at this stage. And again, when the crisis occurs to which reference has been made in Chapter VI (the breakdown of the practice of 'prayerful pondering'), or when symptoms suggestive of this crisis present themselves, we are neither — as a rule — in a position to make the requisite diagnosis, nor are we likely to see for ourselves, or to have the confidence to adopt, the line of prayer which we ought now to be learning to follow. A few words of advice, information, and encouragement in these circumstances can both relieve and shorten our sufferings, and can make them more serviceable to our real progress in prayer.

At other times there will as a rule be less need of a director. Our technological age is so taken up with techniques and technical efficiency that it may be worth while to remind the reader that technique has little to do with prayer; or rather that prayer is the sort of supremely personal activity that requires a technique differing from individual to individual, and that the will to pray will discover for each of us the

---

[4]*Manual for Interior Souls*, pp. 128, 129. The reader will note the touch of rhetoric in 'nothing is more important', and the convention of speaking of 'souls' when one means 'people'.

appropriate 'technique', just as human love discovers the appropriate technique for the inter-personal communion of the lover and his beloved. When, with the help of books and advice, a person has found the mode of prayer which, at least for the present, suits his own call from God, he will rarely need to consult a director about details; and unnecessary discussion about these matters is spiritually enervating. He will, perhaps, somewhat more frequently, need to seek a word of advice about the adaptation of the rest of his life to his prayer. Such consultation is especially desirable when he is considering a major practical change, such as giving up some form of innocent recreation, or even changing from the life of a layman to that of the priesthood or the cloister. At all times it is good to have a director available, and one who knows us well.

The choice of a spiritual guide is a matter of some moment. The guide need not be the priest to whom one usually goes for sacramental absolution. It is often convenient that these two functions should be combined, but it is not necessary, and in some cases is positively undesirable. The guide need not be a clergyman, and in some cases may be a woman. St Teresa of Avila springs to the mind as a woman admirably adapted to guide others (though not, therefore, necessarily to guide herself); and many Mother Superiors are similarly well qualified. It should, however, be observed that in a religious community, a school or a college, there are great disadvantages that may ensue from the guide being a person who has disciplinary authority over the person seeking guidance. The external government of a community is an entirely different thing from interior and personal spiritual direction of the individual members of the community. The two functions call for different qualities, and there is danger in the confusion of the two sorts of authority.

Father Grou lays it down that a director should himself be a man of prayer, a man well versed in spiritual things, as much by his own experience as by study and reading; that he should 'have no purely natural designs, either of vanity or self-interest, but that he should consider only the glory of God and the good of souls; that he should judge of the things of God by the spirit of God'. He adds, rather dryly: 'From all this it is easy to conclude that true directors are very rare.'[5]

An important question arises as to the extent of the 'obedience' which is due to a director. We have already seen that some Indian sects teach that the *guru*, once selected, is to be obeyed implicitly throughout life. Somewhat similarly, Father Grou says that we should show to our director 'a measureless obedience in all those things which cost us the most' and that we should 'never allow ourselves any formal resistance to his will . . . I have spoken elsewhere of obedience; so I will only say here that it cannot be carried too far' (*op. cit.*, p. 133). On the other hand, he allows that our choice of a director may prove to have been mistaken; and in that case, he holds, we shall soon discover that we have made a mistake and 'God will guide us elsewhere' (*ibid.*, p. 132).

I think Grou's teaching on this point is exaggerated, if it is taken to be of general application. There is one class of people, indeed, who must certainly practise 'measureless obedience' to a good and wisely chosen director. These are the scrupulous. Scrupulosity, which may often have a basis in psychological illness, is an abnormal and incapacitating fear of incurring

---

[5]*Manual for Interior Souls*, pp. 128f.

guilt; and it may relate to only one or some departments of the moral life, or (in bad cases) it may be generalised. A person must be prepared to accept the verdict of a good and wise Catholic director that he is scrupulous; and must then consent to substitute his director's judgment for his own over the whole extent of the field in which his scrupulosity operates. And he must especially beware of seeking to get a confirmation or reversal of his director's advice from another quarter. This practice of obedience to his director, in the matters about which he is scrupulous, must be continued till the director expresses himself as satisfied that a cure has been effected —which may not occur before death.

Leaving aside, however, the needs of the scrupulous, it must, I think, be said that the authority of a director is something quite other than the authority of external government. A citizen owes obedience to the civil powers, and a Christian owes obedience to the jurisdiction of the Church. In particular, a monk or nun owes that obedience to his or her religious superiors which is involved in the vows of religious life; ultimately, this is a form of obedience to the Church, from whom all religious superiors derive their governmental authority. In all these cases, obedience is due to the representatives of society, because society is a divinely willed condition of human life. This kind of obedience is not optional.[6]

There is no law of God or man requiring me to have a spiritual director. Hence, the extent of my submission to my

---

[6]It is true that a monk or nun has freely chosen to take the vows which entail obedience. But having taken them, he or she is obliged to obey his or her religious superiors in view of the authority which has been delegated to them by the Church. Similarly, a man is free to marry; but having married, he is bound by the moral obligations implicit in the married state.

director's guidance is to be determined by myself, from whom
his authority over me derives. To surrender my judgment to
him unconditionally (supposing that I am not scrupulous)
would be an immoral act. And should it turn out that the
director whom I have selected requires such unconditional
obedience — still more if he requires me to promise such
obedience — this is an indubitable sign that I have been
mistaken in my choice, and I must reverse it.

On the other hand, it would clearly be absurd to choose a
director with the intention of never following his advice
except when it happened to agree with my own view of a
situation, as formed before I consulted him on it. Nor is a
director to be regarded as enjoying no status other than that of
any other adviser whom I might chance to consult on a given
point. I have chosen him partly as I might choose my lawyer,
doctor, or financial adviser; and partly because, in that
extremely personal region of decision that is the field of moral
and spiritual choice, a person is rarely an impartial judge of his
own case. If I disregard the deliberate advice of my doctor on a
matter of health, I do so at my own peril; and much the same is
true, proportionately, if I disregard the advice of my spiritual
director.[7]

I have said above that an unconditional surrender of one's
judgment to a director — provided one is not scrupulous —

[7]It should perhaps be pointed out here that, in those cases where the director is also the
priest in the confessional, he has an authority as confessor which is other than his
authority as director. His authority as confessor derives from the Church and from Christ.
He may, as confessor, have to exact obedience in a given matter (e.g. reparation in the case
of injury done to another, or avoidance of situations which are likely to lead the penitent
into grave sin) as the price of absolution. As confessor, then, his authority is of different
provenance from his authority as director, and is not subject to the same limitations.

would be immoral. An elaboration of the deepest reason for this proposition may help to throw light on the nature and extent of the docility which is to be shown to a good director.

Religion is man's willed relationship to God. The will is a spiritual faculty, unique in each of us. No one can stand proxy for the will of another (sane) adult. But the will can only act on information provided by the knowing faculties, and especially by the intellect. The intellect, in its turn, is a spiritual and entirely personal faculty. The intellect has to inform the will of the actual situation in which the will is to act. And no other human being can see my situation in all its unique richness. In a religious issue, therefore, as in all moral issues, the determining factor must be my own intellect and my own will.

Moreover, in fact, man has been called by God to a goal, to be attained by man's willed consent, which is above and beyond the scope of our unaided intellects and wills. So that we may be able to make for this goal, he has informed our intellects with the mysteries of faith; and he has given us interior grace, which is not only a strength to our will but an enlightenment to our mind: the light of the Holy Spirit. The supreme and strictly incomparable spiritual director is thus the Holy Spirit, enlightening the mind from within. No step which we take can bring us forward on our path to complete union with God, unless it is taken in obedience to this interior light. So true is this, that it is only by such following of the interior light that we can profitably assent to the mysteries of faith or give our obedience to the authority of the Church. We do not (speaking strictly and precisely) believe because the Bible 'says so', nor obey because the Church bids us do so. We believe and we obey because the Holy Spirit within us bids us to assent to God's revelation and to obey his Church. He bids us believe without limit the full scope of the revelation, and to obey without reserve the authority which Christ has given to his Church. But the ultimate worth of our belief and our obedience is derived from the interior grace and light of the Holy Ghost within us. This light is what enables our conscience to judge aright, and this grace is what enables our will to correspond.

The light of the Holy Spirit directs us to obey the definitely universal moral and spiritual teaching of the Church, because the Church is infallible in such teaching. But no human director is infallible, and it cannot be assumed that the pronouncements of a fallible director will always coincide with the interior guidance of the Holy Spirit. Where they differ, the advice of the human guide must be rejected in favour of God's interior intimations.

There are practical consequences of these truths for the director and for the directed. Having chosen my director with prayerful care, I shall of course respect his advice. I shall normally follow it, and normally I shall have an interior deep-down conviction that I am right to follow it. I shall only not do so if, reluctantly but with a deep and quiet conviction, I feel sure that the advice is wrong for me in my given circumstances; and in such a case it is usually well to tell the director that I do not intend to follow his advice.

The director, for his part, will accept his task with some reluctance and with confidence in God rather than in himself. He will rarely (when not dealing with a scrupulous person) couch his pronouncements in the form of commands, but will prefer the accents of persuasion. His purpose will be, in Father Grou's excellent words, to teach his disciple 'to listen for the divine inspiration, and to respond to it'. He should aim at making himself, so far as may be, no longer necessary to the disciple's spiritual progress. Both he and the disciple must beware of allowing any natural sentiments to sully the purely spiritual relationship of director and disciple. They may both learn from the history of the relations between St Francis de Sales and St Jane Frances Chantal. In the early stages of this relationship he rescued her from the clutches of a director who was tyrannising over her spirit. He then directed her for many years, learning incidentally almost as much as he taught. There was a close human friendship between them, but both knew that this must not contaminate the purely spiritual relationship. And at the last he told her that the time had come for her to get on without him. This decision was heart-breaking, but was accepted with the same simplicity with which it was conveyed by him to her. It helped to make perfect in her that unlimited abandonment to God and his guidance which is the essence of holiness.

It is prudent to look out for a good director, and having found one to make a good use of him. But should it not be possible to find one, or should circumstances arise in which the relationship can no longer be continued, we must remember that nothing that is outside our own control can militate against our progress towards closer union with God — provided we are faithful to grace and the interior light. 'All things work together unto good to them that love God' (Romans viii. 28); all things, including the inability to find a director to whom one can safely turn, and the loss of one when found. In the last resort, my relationship with God is tied to no earthly conditions except that loyalty to revelation and the Church which God himself ordains and makes possible for me.[8]

[8]There are some who, in or out of prayer, think (and are perhaps convinced) that they have received some special revelation of truth or disclosure of God's particular will. Normally, such supposed revelations or disclosures should be simply disregarded. In no case should they be accepted without the concurrence of the director, or, if one has no director, a fully qualified representative of the Church.

ix

Life as Prayer

To discover prayer is to have discovered a new dimension of human living, a gateway out of the high-walled garden of the world's concerns into the open country of the love of God. For this new dimension we were made, and when we awake to its existence we know that it was for this that our heart dumbly sighed in the days of our imprisonment:

> We sat down by the streams of Babylon and wept there, remembering Sion.
>
> Jerusalem, if I forget thee, perish the skill of my right hand! Let my tongue stick fast to the roof of my mouth if I cease to remember thee, if I find in aught but Jerusalem the fountain-head of my content![1]

Did we 'remember Sion'? Or was it that our heart was craving for something that had never been ours and yet had always been appealing secretly to us?

[1] Psalm cxxxvi. 1, 5f.

We were made for joy. There are joys of this life, piercing and transitory. But they speak to us, if our spiritual ear is attuned to their message, of a joy that is so far beyond this life that it can enter in and transform this life and its joys without losing its own transcendent purity.

The joy of prayer is indeed a strange joy. It is compatible with happiness as the world understands happiness. It is also compatible with desolation. Its deepest essence in this life between the cradle and the grave is the peace of certainty; the certainty that the goal to which prayer tends is that Absolute Reality which alone gives meaning and worth to everything that is limited and relative.

A strange joy. And a strange peace; a peace that is sometimes almost imperceptible at the centre of such storms as in our worldiness we had not conceived to be possible. Yet the peace is real, and, as prayer begins to become an inward serenity, not always quite hidden from the onlookers.

We have already seen that prayer stands in a double relationship to the rest of our life. Its fruitful development presupposes some adaptation of the rest of life to the implications of prayer; it is not easy to say, and mean, that we love God with all our hearts when, in the rest of our life, we are making no effort to act in accordance with that love. And on the other hand, prayer tends to accomplish in the rest of life that adaptation which its own development presupposes. It does this both because all real prayer is implicitly or virtually a petition to God to take complete possession of our lives (and God hears and answers the prayer of the humble man), and because real prayer is the vital act of a soul in grace, and grace grows intrinsically stronger by exercise.

The key to that adaptation of life to the implications of prayer which is presupposed by the full development of the life of prayer is the decision, of which we have spoken in Chapter V, 'to do and to suffer, without exception or reserve, everything which is the will of God'. This may seem a formidable resolution; and such, no doubt, to our self-centredness it is. It involves a launching out on an uncharted ocean of action and suffering which our fear of the unknown peoples with bogies. On the other hand, it is a perfectly reasonable decision. It puts us once for all, if we remain faithful, into the safe-keeping of God. And it is a very simple step to take, a mere interior self-determination of our will; it is like the 'yes' which turns a love-affair into an engagement. Certainly, it is an act which we can only perform with the help of God's grace; but no less certainly it is an act for which God will give us the grace if we ask him.

If the habit of, will flowing from this decision is the presupposition of the full development of prayer, what is the essence of prayer? We have seen that it is the intention to devote the period set apart for prayer to a loving attention to God. Behind this intention there lies our knowledge that God wishes us to pray, and that (just for this period of time) that is all that he is asking of us.

Thus our praying is a putting into act, in particular circumstances, of our general resolution to do and suffer whatever God wills. To this extent it is of the same moral texture as our working, our playing, our ordinary human intercourse. Its value for us (and for God) is not the experiences which it may or may not bring with it. Its value lies precisely in the fact that it is what God wishes us to be doing at this moment, and that we are doing it. The next moment may bring another call, to leave immediate 'prayer' for some duty or recreation which is equally (now) God's will for us. Faced by such a call, we should no longer be 'doing or suffering whatever God wills' if we did not turn aside from direct prayer to find God's will, and therefore God himself, elsewhere.

In accepting God's will we 'accept' God, and nowhere else can we find him than in his will. If we do what we do, and suffer what we suffer, because it is God's will, then whatever we do or suffer, all our behaviour and all our experience, is a communion with God.

In so far as we perform our actions, and accept our experiences, *as* the will of God for us, we are attending to God, and 'intending God', in all that we do and all that happens to us. But prayer is the intention of attending to God. Thus, not only is our direct prayer one expression of a life devoted to God, but the rest of our life is a sort of prayer —call it indirect prayer if you like. The only difference between direct and indirect prayer is that, in the former, our task is to forget all that is not God himself, while in the latter our task is to intend God in our deliberate concern with other things. When the books[2] speak of 'continual prayer', they mean this profound harmony, homogeneity, between direct prayer and the rest of our life. None of us can be directly praying all the time:

> How then, and by what kind of prayer, can we fulfil the intentions of our Lord and Master? By the prayer of the heart, which consists of an habitual and constant disposition of love to God, of trust in Him, of resignation to His will in all the

[2]Cf.. for instance, Grou, *Manual for Interior Souls*, pp. 262ff.

events of our lives; in a constant attention to the voice of God, speaking to us in the depths of our consciences and unceasingly suggesting to us thoughts and desires of good and perfection.[3]

The 'continual attention to the voice of God' speaking in our conscience cannot, once again, be continual actual attention with our surface consciousness. But it can be something very real. It can be a sensitiveness to the opportunities, presented by circumstances, of doing something for God; and a sensitiveness to inward impulses to such actions. It is less similar to ordinary 'continual attention' than to the state of mind and will of a mother, working or reading by the cradle of her sleeping child. The mother will not be continually attending (with the surface of her mind) to the child; but the slightest sign of a threat to the child's peace or safety will at once make her alert. This proves that she is continuously united to her child by a strong love in the depths of her being.

Indirect prayer, then, is equivalent to the profound intention governing the whole of our lives. When we have given ourselves to God, and renewed the gift again and again, and when we are habitually making serious efforts to translate this gift into act, we need not be constantly examining ourselves to discover that the intention is present and operative. A mother does not need to ask herself whether she still loves her child. The love of God, when it has taken root in our being, is a sturdy plant. It could not cease without our being keenly aware of the consequent upheaval in our whole interior orientation. True, we are frailty itself, and may expect to fall short very frequently of the full implications of our love for

[3]*Ibid.,* p. 263.

God. But as our prayer and our union with God develop, we shall be more immediately aware of these lapses, we shall more deeply deplore them, and they will be more rapidly consumed in the fire that burns within us.

The human quest for unity may take an intellectual form. In this form it has given rise to the ancient creation myths and the myths of legends of the culture heroes, while at a later date it became the inspiration of Greek philosophy from Thales, who identified the single principle of all things with water, to Plotinus with his doctrine of the 'transcendent first principle, the One or Good'.[4] But the quest may also take a practical form, when it becomes an attempt to achieve a unification of the diverse and divergent impulses and objects of human appetite and will, a unification through identification of the Supreme Good, and through the choice of this Good. Apart from such unification man can never be happy, his personal perfection can never be achieved, his value for himself, for the world, and for Reality must always remain ambiguous.

Nature has endowed man with an intelligence capable of asking ultimate questions and incapable of finding ultimate repose in anything less than the final answers. Correspondingly, a person's will cannot give itself entirely and without remorse except to the unlimited Good. In other words, man is so made as to find supreme and complete happiness in a union of mind and will with God.

Such a union is the goal towards which prayer at its highest is directed. It seeks it less as the condition of our human happiness than because it is what God wills for us. This union is the goal not only of direct prayer but of what we have called

[4] A. H. Armstrong, *Plotinus*, p. 27.

indirect prayer; and it is precisely because every element and aspect of our life can be made subservient to this goal that the life of prayer, life *as* prayer, is the answer here on earth to the human quest of unity.

But always, while we remain on earth, the union with God which can, by grace, be achieved is a union under the veils of faith, a union therefore in darkness, a union with the 'known Unknown'. We believe that this union in faith is but a foretaste, a mysterious but real anticipation, of a union in the light of full knowledge, unclouded intellectual vision. God, whose love created us when we were nothing, and redeemed us after our fall, has planted in us at baptism the seed of faith. The life of prayer is the development of that seed; and of the plant of this life of prayer everlasting vision will be the fruit.

We are all called to the everlasting vision, to find therein the answer to all questionings, the satisfaction of all worthy desire. Joy in the unfailing possession of the infinite Other becomes at last our own. And because we are called to the vision, we are called to become people of faith here and now, and therefore people of that prayer, direct and indirect, which is the development of the seed of faith. It is completely untrue that the life of prayer is the perquisite of a favoured elite or of the professionally devout. It is completely untrue that it presupposes special mental endowments. It is completely untrue that it is incompatible with any legitimate human career or vocation or situation. The infinite love and mercy of God seek us out at the level of our universal human condition, at the level of our common fallenness and of our own individual burden of guilt and past failure. Divine love asks of us one thing only, the one and only thing that love, by its own intrinsic nature, must ask. It asks for the response of our consent to embrace our destiny of everlasting friendship and union with God, who is infinite love, infinite love offering Itself in its infinity to each of us personally.

We can refuse that consent. It is a consent which, by the nature of love and friendship, can only be given freely; and for us, that means that it can be withheld. The responsibility for such refusal would be ours and ours alone.

On the other hand, we can give our consent. We cannot give it except in the power of divine grace, but that grace is offered along with the divine invitation. If, by grace, we give our first consent, then the seed of faith begins to grow in us and, because it is a grace of divine friendship, seeks to grow into the life of prayer, into life *as* prayer. Every stage in that growth is a work of grace, every halting of the growth is the effect of our refusal of grace. So we pray, actually or virtually: God, I love you; grant that by your grace I may no longer shrink from surrendering myself wholly to the current of your love for me.

No one, who realises that the life of prayer is a developing relationship of loving friendship between the one who prays and God, will doubt that prayer must be as various as is the variety of human personalities. There are, however, some broad features that tend to manifest themselves in the progress of most of those who follow the life of prayer. One of these is the gradual transition, both in prayer and in the rest of life, from a stage in which the human activity and effort seem to preponderate to a further stage in which prayer and life seem to become a matter of acceptance rather than of effort. We have to learn the habit of prayer, and like other habits it is acquired by practice and by trying. The young pianist has to 'practise'. We become just, says Aristotle, that is to say we acquire the habit of justice, by doing just actions. So too, for most of us, prayer begins by being something that we laboriously learn and strenuously practise. If there is no universal 'art' or technique of prayer, each of us has, nevertheless, to evolve a technique of his own, and to modify the technique according to the requirements of our own development.[5]

Obviously, too, the process of adapting the rest of our life to the implications of our prayer will at first, for most of us, have been a matter of moral effort and deliberate reorganisation. There will have been things to alter in our ordinary behaviour; passions and affections to control or regulate; sacrifices, it may be, to be determined on and carried into effect. Although in all this, as also in the most elementary prayer, it is the grace of God that is secretly at work within us, still our own contribution, by way of conscious thought and voluntary effort, will have been marked and manifest. At this stage, even our acceptance of the arrangements of divine providence will be an affair of strenuous self-control.

There comes a time, however, or it may come, when the pianist can sit at his instrument and the music seems to flow from his fingers spontaneously; when new creations of musical beauty seem to impose themselves upon his mind and hands while he himself contributes only his non-resistance to the inspiration. So too, Aristotle's 'just man' will grasp without reasoning the moral implications of his situation and will respond, as though impromptu, with an 'act of justice'.

In the development of prayer, the watershed between these two stages may be associated with the resolution of 'devetion'

---

[5]It must be observed, that we are only speaking of what more often occurs. Some people appear to 'discover' prayer, and their own way of praying, in a flash.

which we have dealt with in a previous chapter. That resolution itself is, in fact, rather an acceptance of a situation in
which God is simply asking for our whole love than an
effortful self-adjustment, though its consequences may still
have to be worked out in life with painful effort. Colonel Van
der Post even thought that his decision to 'go and find the
Bushman' was something that had 'happened to him'; but its
consequence was a great deal of planning and a vast deal of
persevering effort. Still, once the resolution of 'devotion' has
been fully and decisively made, it is likely that life will
gradually become far less a matter of self-initiated planning
and effort, far more a matter of consenting to what is inevitable
unless we are to give up our willed relationship with God. To
that extent, we are becoming more 'passive' in our life.

And as our life becomes more passive, so too our prayer
may cease to be so much what we are 'doing' with our set
periods of prayer, and begin gradually to become rather what
we allow God to make of those periods for us. Only we have to
remember that God himself can do nothing for us unless our
consent to his operations is steadily forthcoming. This consent
is essentially identical with our intention to pray.

These pages have been written for those who want some
guidance on the path of prayer. The time may come when no
human guidance or comfort will seem to touch their needs.
This will be because God has set grace to work on the
concluding stages of the 'making of their souls'. Of these stages
we can indeed get some hint from those who have in part
experienced them. Often, it would seem, they involve the
apparent collapse of all that supported, on a human view of
things, their faith or hope or love. Faced with this collapse,
what could they do but fall into the very arms of God? 'It is a

fearful thing', says the Epistle to the Hebrews, 'to fall into the hands of the living God.' Fearful for the one who has deliberately refused that friendship which is the supreme human good, the end for which he was made and to which he was invited, that friendship which even God cannot give him unless he accepts it. For the saint, too, it is 'fearful' to have to fall into God's arms; fearful for all that remains in him of his proud independence and his self-centredness. But the saint needs neither our sympathy nor our advice. He knows, deeper than all his anguish, what is asked of him now; and the obverse of this final surrender is his own joyful secret, and God's.

Appendix

Mystical Prayer[1]

Both components of this paper's title require some explanation. Prayer for many people seems to connote little more than petition; whereas we shall take the broader meaning, that it is a lifting up of the mind and heart to God. The word 'mystical' is very hard to pin down to a fixed meaning. For some, as for Dom Louismet, it is applicable to every stage of the spiritual life from the moment when a Christian starts deliberately out upon the way of perfection. Others appear to take it for granted that the data of mysticism are abnormal. Others again would deny that mysticism is in itself abnormal at all, though some of these would go on to affirm that it is something very infrequent or unusual, and not necessary to holiness. Still

[1]The substance of the following pages was given as a paper to the Catholic Conference of Higher Studies, Easter, 1953. I hope that this may explain the informality of style, and may excuse the rather high-sounding title, which was not my own choice. (Reprinted with permission from *The Clergy Review*, August, 1953.)

others will say that although mystical prayer is something of a very high order, and quite beyond the normal reach of the beginner, yet no Christian life is fully mature till the mystical stage has been attained. Is it unfair to conclude that we can make the word 'mystical' mean anything we like, provided we make clear what we do mean by it? At any rate I hope that there is enough allowed variety of interpretation to cover the view that I wish to develop in these pages.

Although I am supposed to be speaking about prayer, I want to emphasise that the prayer-life of a Christian cannot be studied satisfactorily apart from his spiritual life as a whole. Psychology may be interested in so-called 'phenomena of mysticism' for their own sake. But the theologian's study is dominated by his supreme object, which is God revealed as the saviour of mankind. Prayer, if it is to be considered a part, and not the whole, of the spiritual life, is an aspect of man's response to that object, a response which is both a knowing and a willing, is knowledge and love. It may therefore be expected that as a man's spiritual life as a whole progresses, or fails to progress, so it will be with his prayer-life. And of course, to a certain extent, the reverse is true also: as a person's prayer-life develops, so too will his spiritual life as a whole; if only because prayer is one of the ordinary means of grace.

In the course of the following discussion I wish to draw your attention to a typical crisis in the spiritual life, to the guidance to be given in this crisis, and to the new spiritual conditions that arise when it has been successfully passed. You will realise, however, that the story of each soul is unique, that few human beings 'conform to type' except in the very broadest sense, and that the symptoms of the crisis will vary both from soul to soul and from one kind of vocation to another. I should expect that an agricultural labourer or a city bank clerk will have to pass through the crisis no less than a Carmelite nun; but the external picture of what is going on may differ considerably in these various cases.

I presuppose that the Christian in whom we are at the moment interested is a devout Christian; by which I do not mean a 'pious person'. Nor are we immediately concerned with those habitually in a state of grave sin. Nor, again, are we considering those who, while firmly resolved to remain in a state of grace, are deliberately attached to habits of venial sin; their mental attitude amounts to this: I have not lost the friendship of God, nor therefore the prospect of heaven, so long as I avoid mortal sin; and win the friendship of God and the prospect of heaven I am content.

A great step forward has been taken when all deliberate attachment to venial sin has been renounced; and this is what we may hope is true of the frequent communicant. But a Christian is not 'devout', in my meaning of the word, unless he has, with the help of grace, taken the further step of renouncing, so far as in him lies, all deliberate attachment to habitual imperfection of any sort. This is a negative way of saying that a devout person is aiming, so far as lies within his power with the help of grace, at the perfection of the love of God. 'True and solid devotion', says Grou,[2] 'is that disposition of the heart by which we are ready to do and suffer, without exception or reserve, everything which . . . is the will of God.' The keywords here are 'without exception or reserve' — so many of us make one, or a few, exceptions in our surrender to God's will. Grou points out that this disposition can always go

---

[2] *Manual for Interior Souls*, p. 1.

on increasing 'either in itself or in its effects'. But in its minimal form it is within the powers of a soul in the state of grace, with the help of the actual graces which God will not fail to supply. This disposition is not an infallible prophylactic against sin; but if the devout person falls into sin he can recover his 'devotion' after repenting. It will be seen, then, that there is nothing essentially emotional about this kind of devotion; it is a habit of will.

The devout Christian is aiming at the perfect love of God. He will therefore wish to make due use of the ordinary means of grace. He will need little encouragement to become, if circumstances make it possible and not too difficult, a frequent or even a daily assistant at Mass and communicant. He should be advised to go regularly and fairly frequently to confession. I say 'advised'; and I would point out how important it is for a devout person to have a spiritual director, not merely a priest or priests to absolve. And therefore the clerical student should be trained for spiritual directing by the study of what is called ascetical and mystical theology, and should seek to become himself a spiritual man, so as to be able to give to others something of what he has himself received.

There seems to be no difficulty in principle about this matter of frequenting the sacraments; where circumstances prevent it the practice of spiritual communion should be taught and encouraged. But the other ordinary means of grace, namely prayer, is perhaps too much neglected today. Yet it is in the practice of prayer that there is room for unlimited spiritual progress.

The devout person may need to be taught that the love of God presupposes the knowledge of God in Christ. The quest of such knowledge leads to spiritual reading, especially prayerful Bible reading, and to 'meditation'. As I dislike jargon I would explain that by meditation I here mean prayerful pondering over the mysteries of our redemption, the scenes and discourses of the Gospels, the teaching of St Paul and St John, and so on. By such reading and meditation the devout person, guided by the Holy Spirit, gradually forms within himself a 'picture' of Christ, and 'idea' of God in Christ, which bear some proportion to his general, and especially his spiritual, maturity. How many Christians, with an adult grasp of secular culture, retain a nursery picture of Christ as 'the gentle Jesus, meek and mild', imagined as an insipid bearded shepherd wearing a sort of alb — and accompanied probably by sheep more insipid than himself? How many have an idea of God which is an incongruous fusion of an 'ex-officio explanation of all things' and a secret policeman?

There is nothing particularly recondite or esoteric about meditation. We often meditate about our absent loved ones. And when by imagination and thought they are vividly recalled to our minds we wish that we could speak with them. When the same point is reached in our religious meditation our faith reminds us that God is present everywhere, more present to us than we are to ourselves; and so meditation leads to conversation (not necessarily in words) with God. For many people this conversation is much easier if the meditation takes place during a visit to the Blessed Sacrament. If such visits are impracticable, then meditation can be made when Mass is being attended out of 'devotion'.

How long should be spent daily in meditation and this prayer of conversation? Plainly, no general rule can be laid down; so much depends on the time available, not to speak of the temperament of the individual. If a half-hour daily is a minimum for a priest, it might be argued that a lay person, with all the distractions of modern life to occupy his mind, will need a considerably longer period because he will find it so much harder to 'recollect himself'. Personally, I think the director should be delighted if he can persuade a beginner to spend not less than ten minutes daily at this exercise. The important thing is that, at the early stage, the practice should never be omitted, not even for a single day, unless circumstances are quite abnormally difficult on some particular day. And the tendency should be to increase, within reasonable limits, the time given to it daily. Abbot Cuthbert Butler used to encourage monks to spend two half-hours daily in mental prayer. This is obviously an excellent idea, especially as the distractions of the world invade the modern cloister. But it must be understood that lay people are often hard put to it to secure even a much shorter daily period of quiet for this purpose.

The practice of meditation being once begun, development may be expected.

(1) At first, the dominant surface motive behind the adoption of the practice may have been to seek light, encouragement and grace for the better conduct of one's active life, the acquistion of virtues, and the struggle against self-love. Looked at in this way, meditation is a weapon in the spiritual combat. But the conversation with God will probably come to seem unimportant in and for itself. If holiness is a union of mind and will with God, such conversation is itself an exercise of union. By degrees the devout person may come to a frame of mind in which he is not so much trying to pray well in order to live well, as trying to live better in order to pray better.

Doubtless in fact life and prayer are influencing each other all along.

(2) There will probably be a tendency to spend more of the allotted time in conversation with God and less therefore in meditation ('prayerful pondering'). From the very early stages it should be realised that praying is better than thinking about the things of God. But as the element of meditation diminishes in the time set apart for prayer, the devout person should be encouraged to make up for it by a regular practice of spiritual reading at some other time of the day. Spiritual reading is a great, and on the whole necessary, antidote to the unchristian and antichristian suggestions that meet us at every turn today.

(3) The conversation with God may tend to become simplified. It may tend towards the mental repetition (slowly and peacefully) of a few simple 'acts': O my God I love thee; Heal me, Lord, and I shall be healed, save me and I shall be saved, for thou art my glory; God be merciful to me a sinner; my God, I want thee as I want nothing else; My soul magnifies the Lord and my spirit hath rejoiced in God my saviour; Jesus.

(4) From the first, the devout Christian should be encouraged to make, during his daily period of meditation and 'conversation', short pauses of loving attention to God. He may be reminded that moments of silence between friends can be as eloquent as any amount of chatter. It is perhaps dangerous to tell him that conversation is a duologue and that he should give God a chance to have his say; rather he must be warned not to want or expect recognisable 'messages' or 'words' from God, and to take no notice of such if they seem to him to occur. Prayer is a matter of faith, not of prophetic revelations. These short pauses are of great importance,

because they may prove later on to have been the harbingers of the kind of prayer which will become characteristic after the crisis has supervened to which we must now turn our attention.

I take the following imaginary picture from Père Gabriel de Ste Marie-Madeleine's study, *Acquired contemplation* (English translation in *St John of the Cross, Doctor of Divine Love and Contemplation*, Mercier Press, 1946):

> A devout seminarian, 'accustomed to sensibly sweet and ardent love' one day goes faithfully to the chapel at the first sound of the bell for mental prayer. He seems to have walked into an atmosphere which is glacial. He does not know what is the matter, but it is as though, all at once, God has retired to a distance. Since he wants to have Him near him again the good youth returns to his accustomed meditation. He takes up the consideration of a mystery often hitherto a source of great sweetness: the institution of the Eucharist, in the presence of which he has in the past found such great joy. Useless! he cannot succeed in fixing his attention upon the mystery — he cannot string together two holy thoughts! Somewhat depressed, he decides to pass on to the affective [i.e. the volitional] part of his prayer, hoping at least to be able to express his love for God. But here he experiences another difficulty: it is absolutely impossible to move his heart. He remains cold, frozen.

At first the young man thinks that perhaps tomorrow things will go better. For passing bouts of 'dryness' in prayer may occur to anybody; whether physical indisposition, weariness, distracting anxieties, or some infidelity to grace be the explanation. But suppose the 'dryness' proves to be chronic; and suppose that there seems to be no explanation of it in ill-health, sin committed, or other discoverable obstacle to prayer?

We remember that we are, *ex hypothesi*, dealing with a devout person, one, that is, who has been co-operating faithfully with grace. And now (not necessarily suddenly, as P. Gabriel suggests; I think it may be the result of a gradual process whose early stages may be hardly noticed) it is as though the light had gone out. The imagination is barren. Pious thoughts do not come spontaneously and can hardly be forced out of the reasoning mind. The emotions are all cold and lifeless. Christ seems no longer present in the tabernacle, in the external world, in the heart, or even in the moments of absolution and holy communion. And this crisis of prayer may be accompanied by a crisis in the sphere of moral effort: the desire and energy to be good, to grow better, to resist temptation, may seem to be atrophied. Old temptations rear their heads with renewed strength. New creaturely attractions threaten to divert the soul from the love of God. The soul is in darkness, and very likely in dismay.

Yet after hearing this tale of woe from the lips of the sufferer, if the director were to ask him: Well then, do you propose to give up seeking God? I imagine that the reply might be: I no longer quite know what you mean by God, but what else is there to seek for? In other words, the desire, the radical purpose, to attain a closer communion with God is as real as ever, is even intensified by seeming to be temporarily baulked; and the evidence of this is the acute distress of the soul in its unaccustomed darkness.

It is this combination, of an incapacity to 'meditate' and 'talk' with God after faithful practice; of a 'hunger and thirst for the living God'; and of a deep sense of the inadequacy of all creatures, that constitutes the 'sign' for entering upon a new stage of the spiritual life, a stage that is superficially, and perhaps really, very different from that which preceded it. There comes a time, if a soul is faithful to grace, when the Christian makes at any rate some sort of hardly conscious, fumbling, distinction between his idea of God and God the reality; when images and even concepts and considerations cannot satisfy the metaphysical appetite for the real within which sanctifying grace operates.

It will be observed that the 'sign' described in the last paragraph is practically St John of the Cross's 'signs' for the transition to 'obscure contemplation'. Father Copleston, in a recent article,[3] says that he thinks that the saint's point is that 'no one is entitled to make, as it were, experiments in mysticism, out of curiosity or desire to be out of the ordinary. A quiet attraction for the contemplation of the incomprehensible and unimaginable God must first be experienced. For this attraction, when genuine and not artificially produced, is a sign that God is himself leading the soul.'

I wonder whether Father Copleston would accept a few modifications of this statement? I should like to drop the word 'contemplation' from it, preferring to speak of an attraction for 'the unimaginable and incomprehensible God'. Then I would suggest that the existence of this attraction may appear to be doubtful to the person going through these trials; it may be obvious to the director. What the sufferer himself is probably

---

[3]'David Hume and St John of the Cross', *The Month*, August, 1952.

most aware of is the breakdown of his previous way of prayer. This breakdown is in fact due to the more or less concealed growth within him of a desire for God himself beyond images and ideas. His 'taste' is changing; he is 'out' for something, he knows not what, but it is something different from anything you can describe to him. And because imaginations and concepts and sensible emotions and sensible desires fail him, he seems to be in a sort of spiritual fog or darkness and paralysis. What is he to do?

First he should be told that at all costs he must not shorten or give up his times of prayer — what he used to call his meditation. He may feel that this has become a complete waste of time; that it would be better to read a spiritual book or recite a litany of the penitential psalms, or (if he is a priest) to prepare a sermon, or even to go off and do some good work. This is a temptation; the time is not being wasted.

He is to be told that the state in which he finds himself is the result of a grace from God. And his task now, with the help of his director, is to find the kind of behaviour in prayer that fits his present state and call. It is not easy to make out a general prescription, precisely because prayer at this stage is becoming in the fullest sense personal, and every person is unique — you cannot prescribe to another how he is to express his love for the person he is in love with. But in general we may say that he is to seek a tranquil resting of the mind and heart in the presence of God apprehended by faith. Not in the 'sense' of God's presence, which is just what at this stage is often denied to him. But sense or no sense (and for the present the lack of such a sense is probably an advantage) faith teaches him that God is present to him and he to God. He is to seek to cultivate a very peaceful attention to God thus present. If it helps him, he may make an occasional quiet ejaculation or aspiration to God; and the same aspiration, or series of aspirations, may be repeated at intervals. But he is to be encouraged to think of these little bits of formed adoration, thanksgiving, sorrow or petition, not as constituting the heart of his prayer but as its occasional concomitant. If it helps him, he can compare himself with a mother, sitting silent and (at heart) absorbed in love by the cradle of her sleeping child; she needs not to speak, yet her heart is actively loving her child. So he is loving God. His attitude of mind, whether or not it finds verbal expression, may be described as follows: My God, I am nothing, I have nothing. I covet nothing but thee.

I have said that he is to seek to cultivate a very peaceful — and, I would add, loving — attention to God. The word 'attention' may serve to introduce the subject of distractions, which for many may be the most marked superficial characteristic of this form of prayer. The imagination and the discursive reason are by nature restless; and although the dominant deliberate will may be aiming at God, the appetites may still be craving for their created objects. Hence, just because the soul's need now is for a kind of prayer that relies little, if at all (after the few moments needed to establish the soul at prayer), on imaginations, thoughts and feelings, the 'lower self' (or, to change the metaphor, the 'surface self') may become infected with distracting memories and ideas and imaginations, fed to it by its immortified self-love, or suggested by the quite legitimate occupations of daily life.

Of course, deliberate distractions are incompatible with any very real mental prayer. I am not in any sense trying to attend to 'God alone' if I am deliberately willing to attend to something which takes my heart away from God. All that needs to be said here about fully deliberate distractions is that they are to be eschewed.

The real difficulties arise in connection with distractions that are not fully deliberate. Even among these there are some that are entirely trivial: the sort of vague floating wisps of imagination and thought that can co-exist with profound absorption not only in prayer but outside it —absorption, for instance, in a piece of music to which one is listening. These trivialities can and should simply be disregarded; to attempt to control them is obviously tantamount to abandoning one's absorption. But other involuntary distractions appear to sweep the self away with them and to destroy anything normally described as absorption in God. They may obsess their victim so habitually that he feels inclined to say that he 'cannot pray'. He goes faithfully to his habitual place of prayer, his prie-dieu, the chapel of the Blessed Sacrament, the cloister or the garden walk; he makes the sign of the Cross and an act of faith in God's presence; he offers to God the coming half-hour (or hour, or quarter of an hour) — and a few minutes later he realises that he has been, for minutes on end, pursuing a line of thought that is completely irrelevant. He recovers himself and forms an aspiration or 'renews his attention'; and the same thing happens again. The set time for prayer runs to its end (he must be warned not to try to make up by extending the period allotted) and apparently virtually nothing has been accomplished. It is natural that he should complain: I cannot pray.

You may think that what I have just been describing, though regrettably common, is anything but mystical. I am not particularly in love with the word, but I would not underrate the value of this distracted prayer. The distractions in question are not fully deliberate. This means that, insistent

and persistent though they may be, they have not caused, nor
are they the effect of, a diversion of the fully deliberate will. By
setting aside this half-hour for prayer, when it might have
been given to recreation or to interesting or urgent business,
by devoting it to prayer and persevering in an apparently futile
attempt at prayer for the full half-hour, I have expressed and
put into operation my intention to pray. And as my distractions were not fully deliberate I have not retracted that
intention. Indeed, from time to time, as I became aware of the
distractions and turned from them, I at least virtually renewed
my intention to pray.

The proposition which I wish to submit to you is that the
essence of pure prayer, or at least the essence of what we
contribute to pure prayer, is the real intention to pray. It is of
course obvious that, where there is no such intention, there is
no prayer. But I am contending for the contrary proposition,
that prayer is essentially not (of course) of the imagination;
that it is not of the discursive reason; nor even of actual
attention; but that it is of real intention. It is the voluntary
direction of the self at its highest (or deepest) level, a level
beyond our normal capacity for reflection upon our acts,
towards God the supreme reality, as apprehended by faith.

Sanctifying grace gives us a habitual inclination towards
God in the 'apex of the soul'. Prayer is the actuation of that
inclination in an intention to attend lovingly to God. That in
fact we seem to attend hardly at all does not in the least
invalidate our intention. Where that intention is present
—and surely it is present in our daily mental prayer unless it
is actually retracted — there is prayer; and there, when
imaginative, discursive and articulate prayer fails us, is, I
would suggest, at least the beginnings of mystical prayer.

Various questions arise in connection with this crisis of prayer; a crisis which I take to be a crisis of general spiritual development. (1) Is it the normal lot of all devout Christians to have to pass through such a crisis? (*a*) I should begin my reply to this question by suggesting that the classical descriptions of the crisis may be coloured by the fact that the masters (and mistresses) of mystical theology have often been religious, not seldom religious of contemplative orders or congregations, and usually writing with special reference to the spiritual development of 'beginners' in such orders or congregations. The picture may have to be varied in many of its superficial features to be applicable to lay people called to an active life in the world. (*b*) The classical picture, as found for instance in St John of the Cross, was elaborated at a time when it was customary to identify devout prayer with formal methodical meditation, and this circumstance tended to make the crisis unnecessarily violent. Later on, as for instance in Caussade's splendid treatise *On Prayer*, a technique was worked out for meditative prayer with a view to facilitating the transition to the prayer of 'loving attention', especially by the encouragement of quiet pauses already in the meditative stage. (*c*) But with these provisos I think that something corresponding to this crisis is normal in the spiritual life, something analogous to the crisis of adolescence in our natural growing-up.

(2) What is the theological explanation of the crisis and the kind of prayer that then supervenes? (*a*) A word first about the psychological explanation: I have already said that I think that this is to be sought in the fact that the devout person in question has reached a point at which imaginations, considerations, emotions, and I would add particular acts of 'discursive'

willing, are inadequate to his growing desire for God as he is in himself. (*b*) But God as he is in himself can only be attained in so far as he freely gives himself. And indeed the lover of God would not wish it to be otherwise. He would not value God, or union with God, so much as he does if God were not too high for his natural apprehension even when aided by common grace. Bound up with his love is his wonder that he who 'dwells in inaccessible light' should thus draw near to man. 'What is man that thou hast made thyself known to him?' (*c*) It seems therefore that the crisis is caused by an intensified intervention of the Holy Spirit which, pre-supposing the normal activity of faith, hope and charity, plays upon the 'gifts of the Holy Spirit' so as to produce an actuation of the soul in grace which transcends the lower modes of operation of faith, hope and charity with their dependence upon discursive occupation with the material object of faith. (Of course, I only offer this as a tentative note on a profound, and profoundly delicate, topic of theology.)

(3) Is the kind of prayer which I have attempted to describe 'mystical prayer'? I am not sure that I consider the answer to this question very important in itself. If I say that I am inclined to answer 'Yes', it is because I think it desirable that books like *The Cloud of Unknowing*, usually regarded as 'mystical', should be recognised as dealing with this sort of prayer. I would also suggest that this kind of prayer is normal for the vast majority of devout persons (when they have passed the crisis) for possibly most of the rest of their lives. It is St John of the Cross's 'obscure contemplation'. I imagine that St Teresa's 'prayer of quiet' is usually regarded as a stage beyond anything that I have here described or discussed. But I am not convinced that the prayer of quiet *as described by St Teresa* represents a

stage of development that is generally necessary to sanctity. Yet I suspect that as the soul moves on to the level of habitual heroic sanctity there are likely to be episodes like that 'ecstasy' of love described by St Thérèse of Lisieux, of which she said that she felt as if she must die if it continued much longer.

(4) The crisis we have been (most inadequately) considering is what St John of the Cross calls the passive purgation of the senses. It would appear that consummate sanctity presupposes a further, more interior, more painful, 'passive purgation of the spirit' (i.e. of the intellect and will), which is essentially a purification of faith, hope and charity, whereby they are made independent of 'grounds of credibility' and all grounds and motives less than their own essential motive, which is God himself, truth self-revealing, redeemer of the helpless, object of pure love transcending all self-centred interest.

(5) Such are the heights towards which the grace of baptism calls us. I want to suggest that there is truth in a remark of the late Father Steuart S.J., that even in the stages of prayer before the crisis of the passive purgation of the senses there is perhaps 'some adumbration of a definite mystical element in our worship, an obscure but confident reference to the hidden plane of divine reality, a transcendence of the boundaries of reason and imagination, something already of the "luminous faith" of which St John of the Cross speaks'.[4]

How far, if at all, the suggestions made in these pages correspond to the evidence gathered by the pastoral clergy in their direction of the devout persons who turn to them for help is a question to which I should be keenly interested in finding an answer. A *priori* it appears to me that every soul,

---

[4] *The Two Voices*, p. 231.

unless prevented by premature death, ought to develop in the way implied in the following passage of Caussade:

> At one period (sc. before the 'crisis') the soul lives in God, at another God lives in the soul. These two periods have opposite requirements. When God lives in the soul, the soul must commit itself entirely to his providence. When the soul lives in God, it carefully and regularly provides for itself all the means it can think of for attaining to union with God. Its routes are sign-posted, it has its spiritual reading, its examens and its reviews of conduct. Its director is at hand; and everything is laid down by rule, even to hours of talking and silence.
>
> But when God lives in the soul, the soul no longer has anything of itself, but only what it receives from moment to moment from God, its animating principle. It lays up no store for the journey and has no mapped-out route. It is like a child which one leads where one will and which has only its feelings to distinguish the objects presented to it. This soul no longer has assigned books; often it is deprived of a definite director; God leaves it with no support save himself. Its abode is in darkness, oblivion, dereliction, death and nothingness. It feels its needs and miseries, but knows not how or when it will be helped. It waits in peace and without anxiety for help to come; it looks only to heaven. God, who can find no purer disposition in the soul than this total giving-up of all that it is so as to live only by grace and divine operation, provides it according to its need with books, thoughts, insights into itself, advice, counsel, and the example of the wise. . . . Others undertake for God's glory an infinity of things; but this soul, often enough, is abandoned in a corner, like a bit of broken pottery which no one imagines to be of any use. Thus abandoned by creatures, but experiencing God by a very real, true and active love,

though it is a love infused in repose, this soul does not apply itself to anything by its own movement; all it can do is to abandon itself and surrender itself into God's hands, to serve him in ways known to him. Often it does not know how it is serving him, but God knows all right. Men think it useless, and their opinion is supported by appearances. Yet it remains true that by secret influences and unknown channels it radiates an infinity of graces on people who, often, are unaware of it and of whom it is unaware. Everything is efficacious, everything preaches, everything is apostolic, in these abandoned souls . . . God operates in them by unforeseen and often unrecognised impulse — they are like Jesus, from whom proceeded a secret healing power.[5]

It will be recognised that Caussade, in this passage, is painting an idealised picture. The question is whether or not it depicts a real change that comes over all souls as they advance in holiness. Is it, or is it not, true that there comes a stage when the devout soul reaches, so to speak, the end of its own resources alike in prayer, in the struggle against self-love, and in work for others; when the contrast between its ideal and its achievement becomes more than ever painfully apparent to itself, with a pain intensified by a new and growing sense of its own helplessness; when all that remains for it to do is precisely what God wants it to do —to let him take over the controls; to submit without measure; to let itself be possessed by the unfelt certainty of his love; no longer to initiate action but to adapt itself, always (in its own judgment) feebly and inadequately, to his requirements expressed in what look like purely natural and fortuitous circumstances; to recognise at long last that

---

[5]*Abandon à la divine providence,* ii, 1,1.

what you are. matters more than what you do, and indeed determines what you effect; to find itself, in short, helplessly suffering on a cross from which it could at any moment come down, but from which it will not come down because only he who loses his life will find it?

If so, then (I should conclude) all souls are called to the mystical life and to some form of mystical prayer.

I think we need to remind ourselves, and those we teach, that this is the true development of sanctifying grace. The real need of the present day is the age-old need for the deepening of the spiritual life, especially by the encouragement of 'meditation' and personal prayer. We have had our revival of the religious orders, our Thomist renaissance, our exhortation to frequent communion (a tremendously good thing, but not enough by itself), our liturgical movements, our Catholic Action, our general recovery of emphasis upon the corporateness of Christianity. But the life of the Church militant is an 'interior life', is lived in and by the individual members of the Church; and so we come back to 'personal religion', to the unchanging truth that a person cannot serve two masters, to self-conquest and the abandonment of self into the hands of God, to meditation and personal prayer as that which makes more fruitful even our sacramental life, to a 'realisation' of what we all know, namely that the Holy Spirit is the prime agent of the sanctification of the Church in her members and that he is poured into our hearts and there not only makes intercession for us with yearnings incapable of formulation in words, but actually takes our life up into his own life, which is wholly a life of sounding, by contemplation and love, the infinite abyss of the being and truth and love of the Holy Trinity.